"It takes more than wonderful artists to make audiences—and Donna Walker-Kuhne knows ___ strategy isn't 'one free play,' because to her, audience members are more than consumers. They are your collaborators in a creative adventure. Her approach—tapping people's spirits and not just their pocketbooks—is genuinely inspiring and long overdue. Use it and you'll never again play for people who are there only because it's the night they have tickets. You deserve better, and now that Donna Walker-Kuhne has written this book, you can have what you deserve."

—GREGORY MOSHER, *Columbia University;*
Former Artistic Director of Lincoln Center Theater
and The Goodman Theatre

"An African proverb tells us that when spiderwebs connect, they can tie up a lion. A 'lion' of Donna's is developing multicultural audiences and working with college students. From Astor Place to NYU's 4th Street, Donna has spun her web over the years to connect our students to the arts. Now putting her magic into print casts her web even wider. What a vision for helping us to see why arts in education is so powerful in developing new audiences."

—PATRICIA M. CAREY, *Steinhardt Associate Dean &*
University Assistant Chancellor, New York University

"It is always a joyous learning experience to listen to Donna as a conference panelist or as a guest speaker at a theatre industry event or, better yet, on a one-on-one telephone call as she shares her knowledge of developing a diverse audience for today's theatre. In my opinion, no one is more in touch with ways to cultivate the new theatregoer. Donna has traveled all over the country working with presenters with great success throughout her career. Now every theatre professional is 'Invited to the Party' to benefit from Donna's experience."

—ED SANDLER, *Director of Membership Services,*
The League of American Theatres & Producers

Invitation to the Party

Invitation to the Party

BUILDING BRIDGES TO
THE ARTS, CULTURE
AND COMMUNITY

Donna Walker-Kuhne

THEATRE COMMUNICATIONS GROUP
NEW YORK
2005

Invitation to the Party: Building Bridges to the Arts, Culture and Community
is published by Theatre Communications Group, Inc., 520 Eighth Avenue,
24th Floor, New York, NY 10018-4156.

This publication is made possible in part with public funds from
the New York State Council on the Arts, a State Agency.

TCG books are exclusively distributed to the book trade by
Consortium Book Sales and Distribution, 1045 Westgate Dr., St. Paul, MN 55114.

LIBRARY OF CONGRESS CATALOGING-IN-PUBLICATION DATA
Walker-Kuhne, Donna.
Invitation to the party : building bridges to the arts, culture and community /
Donna Walker-Kuhne.— 1st ed.
p. cm.
ISBN-13: 978-1-55936-230-6 (alk. paper)
ISBN-10: 1-55936-230-8 (alk. paper)
1. Performing arts—Audiences. 2. Performing arts—Public relations. I. Title.
PN1590.A9W35 2005
791—dc22   2005020356

Cover design and author photo by Kitty Suen
Text design and composition by Lisa Govan

First Edition, August 2005
Second Printing, November 2007

To

_____

My mother for her unconditional love and faith in me.

*My late father, who created a nest where
I could flourish despite his early passing.*

My sister, Sheila, for her steadfast belief in and passion for the arts.

My twin sister, Patricia, for her constant display of fearlessness.

*My dearest husband, who fuels my constant appreciation of life
and love and whose generosity of spirit enabled me to soar fearlessly
into this endeavor.*

*My spirited daughter, Theresia,
who constantly provides the wonder and joy of life.*

To Daisaku Ikeda for showing me the way.

Acknowledgments

I would like to acknowledge all the incredible mentors in my life who have nourished my desire to be enveloped by art and culture: Carol Folkes, my first ballet teacher; Hermaine Billingslea, who taught me to play the piano with passion; Julian Swain, who taught me African dance and opened the door to performing possibilities; Najwa I, who taught me how to perform, fueled the passion and taught me about my heritage; the late Larry Phillips, who launched my career as an arts administrator; Arthur Mitchell, who took it to new heights; George C. Wolfe who gave me the platform to soar; and the late Amelia Moran for guidance and love.

My family: Aunt Chee-Chee; Aunt Vivian; Daryl Bender; Arletta Bender; my adopted sister, Iris Davis; and other cousins and relatives who make me proud of my bloodline.

Colleagues in the industry who help me develop new strategies and broaden my understanding: Gary Steur, Ben Cameron, the late Ana Araiz, Irene Cabrera, Claudia Chouniard, Charlayne Haynes, Dean Sharon Smith, Lisa Kornisberg, Tracey Mendelsohn, Abiba Wynn, Tiffany Ellis, Monique Martin, Isisara Bey, Marcia Pendelton, Jeri Love, Mikki Shepard, Neyda Martinez, Jean Owensby, Evan Shapiro,

Tobi Stein, Sharon Jensen, Rick Thompson, Sister A'Aliyah Abdul Karim, the late Elizabeth McKinney, Dr. Mildred Clark, Julie Peeler and my assistant and Special Projects Director, Natalie Clarke.

To the encouraging members of the Soka Gakkai International–USA, especially those members in Brooklyn Region, who always empower me by their faith and guidance.

To the many women and men who welcomed me into their hearts while I was touring with both Dance Theatre of Harlem and *Bring in 'Da Noise, Bring in 'Da Funk*.

To the incredible pioneers who have entered into this arena of building audiences with cultural institutions—enduring the pressures of producing results, with minimal resources and large expectations—there are so many of you all around the country. You know who you are. Thank you.

To the hundreds of students with whom I've had the privilege of sharing my thoughts, vision and strategies over the years. Thank you for inspiring me, challenging me and encouraging me to strive for excellence.

To the writers who provided editorial support: Stephanie Coen, for your encouragement from the very beginning; Jeri Love, for showing me what the shape of the book could look like; and my editor at TCG, Kathy Sova, your faith, talent and patience continue to amaze me, you are a love.

Lastly, as I was writing this book, the music of Brasil 66, with Sergio Mendes and Nancy Wilson, took me to a place where I felt safe to open my heart.

Contents

Contents

Introduction

BUILDING BRIDGES TO ARTS, CULTURE AND COMMUNITY

The arts are a response to our individuality
and our nature and help to shape our identity.
The arts are not a frill and should not be
treated as such. They have the potential to
become the driving force for healing division
and divisiveness.

—Barbara Jordan
The late U.S. Representative

I knew I had a story to tell in 1993, when I left Dance Theatre of Harlem to take on the newly created Director of Community Affairs position at The Public Theater in downtown New York City.

As soon as I started this challenging new job, I felt compelled to write this book, because the demand from performing arts producers seeking audiences of color had become intense, and I was fielding constant phone calls and requests for lectures and workshops. The success of the The Public's production, *Bring in 'Da Noise, Bring in 'Da Funk*, and then its transfer to Broadway followed by a successful national tour, drew attention to my ability to deliver results in terms of new audiences and earned income.

There was a growing awareness that diversity was no longer a consideration but a necessity. I was very encouraged. Previously, presenters and producers had thought if they produced an "ethnic" product, that that particular event might be supported by audiences of color, but would not result in crossover into the institution's ongoing programming. They also thought that "community" arts programming would de-value their institution's reputation.

When one suggests that the artistic value of community arts programming is somehow less than fully professional, it reduces the importance of this work. We need to elevate the environment in which this type of art lives, to bring authority to this field. For the past twenty-four years I have been educating presenters (and audiences) about the importance of crossing this bridge, showing them how to integrate the arts in a holistic way into the fabric of an institution.

Through my marketing and audience development work around the country, I've observed that there are very few people who really understand how to embrace different demographics in their marketing strategies. Marketers need to develop a sensitivity to this issue. To be successful, audience development requires a specific strategy. *It is a science.*

This book is intended to guide producers, presenters, arts administrators and educators toward specific strategies that engage, educate and activate (primarily, but not exclusively) audiences of color. It is also a guide for anyone involved in the art of marketing any product who has the wisdom to understand that the world is changing, that there is now, more than ever, a specific need to embrace everyone.

Who are the people we are trying to reach? In 1990, *Time* Magazine published a cover story: "America's Changing Colors," in which it noted that, by 2056, most Americans will trace their descent to Africa, Asia, Latin America, the Pacific Islands or the Middle East. This marks a dramatic change in our nation's ethnic composition. Current social and generational changes are already having an effect. Our potential audiences include new immigrant groups from Asia, Europe, Africa and Latin America; a growing and diverse Latino population; the old and new African American middle class; the hip-hop generation; yuppies; the gay and lesbian community; Generations X and Y, among others. Whether you're engaged in theatre, dance, fine arts, music, the commercial or not-for-profit entertainment industries, the changing demographics of the twenty-first century demand that you change how you do business, not just for the sake of our collective cultures, but for the survival of our institutions. We can no longer expect arts institutions to survive in the long-term without some sophisticated, well-thought-out plan to embrace diverse audiences. There is tremendous competition, which will only increase from our techno society. What role will the arts have?

This is a book about how to engage people who are different from you and create longstanding value from that relationship. It provides a how-to at finding new communities for your theatre, whether they be recent immigrants or well-established communities who rarely venture outside their comfort zone.

Audience development is most effective when it is seen in a philosophical and historical context. There must be a deep understanding as to why this work is necessary in the first place. There must be compassion, a willingness to understand the history of our many disenfranchised communities and their reluctance to embrace unfamiliar experiences, people and products. Before we can discuss strategy, we must always discover who we are working to serve. Who is the audience? Who lives in the community? What is their history, where do they work, how do they spend their time and where? If we expect people to support, enjoy and learn from the arts, we must create an environment that is warm, open and relative to their unique cultural experiences.

I firmly believe that the arts is the only pure vehicle we have in today's society that crosses cultural and ethnic barriers and allows people to transcend their differences. Today, more than ever, the need to clarify misunderstandings, erase social strife and celebrate diversity is vividly apparent. It is through understanding our diversity that we can appreciate our shared humanity.

This book represents my experience in cultivating audiences for theatre, dance, music and the visual arts. It illustrates my work for many wonderful performing arts groups, such as The Thelma Hill Performing Arts Center, Dance Theatre of Harlem and The Public Theater, as well as my work on touring productions and Broadway shows. My experience as a dancer, lawyer, audience development specialist, marketer and college professor has allowed me to work in the arts in a variety of ways. This diverse background has been crucial to the development of my marketing strategies, and has provided me the opportunity to develop audiences for theatres throughout the U.S., Southeast Asia, Australia and North and South Africa.

I don't profess to offer any undiscovered theories. This book is about *doing* it—this is what's new and this is where we will break ground and create history. I illustrate how to get it done: the hiring of staff, the creation of an institutional vision to diversify audiences, the programming that invites new audiences, the sincerity. I want to illuminate the importance and value of inviting communities previously denied to come to the party. Come join me!

Donna Walker-Kuhne
Brooklyn, NY
August 2005

Invitation to
the Party

Chapter 1

YOU MUST BEGIN
WITH A VISION
AND A PLAN

If you don't have a clear picture of your destination and a precise map to get there, you won't even begin the trip.

—Steven K. Scott
Simple Steps to Impossible Dreams

During one of my first meetings with writer and director George C. Wolfe, soon after he was named Producer at The Public Theater/ New York Shakespeare Festival in 1993, he shared his vision for his theatre, one of the country's leading cultural centers: "I want to create a theatre that looks and feels like a subway stop in New York City. I have been here three months and notice that the audiences are predominately white—how would you change it? That's as simple as it is. People might call it multiculturalism or diversity. To me, it's just creat-

3

ing theatre that looks and feels like the people we serve. This theatre is part of a cultural institution that is as committed to serving its community as it is to putting on plays."

The night following my meeting with George, I had a dream that I can, to this day, still see vividly. It took place in the lobby of The Public during a brightly lit party. There were people from all different walks of life, from neighborhoods throughout New York City as well as from all over the world. They were speaking many different languages, but their common bond was joyous laughter and the sharing of a good time. This dream remains the motivation for my work. I replay it in my mind daily, and each day I recommit to taking whatever steps necessary to translate it into a reality.

Since 1993, The Public Theater has expanded its mission to be a theatre where all the country's voices, rhythms and cultures converge. It is a theatre that embraces the complexities of contemporary society and nurtures both artists and audiences through its commitment that The Public should be a place of inclusion and a forum for ideas.

An effective audience development initiative begins with a vision—a dream—and a plan. The more specific and detailed the blueprint you create, the more effective you are going to be. Take a minute and think about this: What is your vision? Is it personal or institutional? What do you need to make it happen? With whom do you share this vision?

The answer to the last question is critical, not only for theatre companies but for all of today's arts institutions. Indeed, it is the basis of a central philosophy of the groundbreaking Lila Wallace-Reader's Digest Fund publication, *Opening the Door to the Entire Community: How Museums Are Using Permanent Collections to Engage Audiences.* The report, published in 1998, was the result of a 7-year, $32-million initiative dedicated to audience-building strategies at 29 museums around the country. Complete institutional investment in the process of community engagement became a mandate of the study. Many of the executive directors and managing directors echoed this sentiment. The report states:

> Chartering a new course for audience development can't just be the passion of a museum's director or its marketing or education department. It requires the commitment of the entire institution to conduct business in new ways that reach far beyond the walls of the museum.

The most important component of audience development is a spirit of collaboration among every department of the arts institution—a willingness to invest the time, labor and resources needed to be successful. That spirit begins at the top, with the management team, board of directors, department heads, etc. Every department and every employee must have a vested interest in the vision and, once united, advance single-mindedly toward that goal. If an institutional leader commits to diversifying audiences because he or she loves the idea (or simply to appeal to a funder) but is not willing to commit staff, creativity or a plan to that process, the objective will fail.

Having a clear vision has made all the difference for some prominent arts institutions. Here are a few examples:

Years ago, the late Alvin Ailey said: "Dance is for everybody. It came from the people; it should always be given back to the people." Since its founding in 1958, the Alvin Ailey American Dance Theater has held fast to this principle. Through its dance school, training programs and commitment to touring, the company has remained fully accessible while maintaining a level of artistic brilliance and excellence that touches its audiences' hearts. Judith Jamison, a heralded former member of the American Dance Theater and its current artistic director, says, "Dance is the language that reveals the heart—the language of approach and convergence, the vocabulary that makes visible our truest selves." She encourages audiences to get to know the company's dancers, whose fearlessness and grace is astonishing. Though the company's composition is international, it has remained true to its original mandate to promote the uniqueness of black cultural expression and showcase the works of black choreographers. The company has displayed agility in retaining its identity, while uniting all people in dance. It has also remained true to its commitment to promote and present its art to underserved communities.

Another wonderful example of staying true to a mission is the Old Town School of Folk Music in Chicago, IL, which was founded in 1957. I believe Jim Hirsch (former executive director) exemplifies what it means to be a visionary. This institution has a community outreach department and a mission statement that reads: "The mission of the Old Town School of Folk Music is to serve as a local and national resource for the teaching, presentation and encouragement of folk music and folk culture of all countries; to collect, preserve and display folk music and folk-related materials; and to introduce folk music to new audiences of all ages, cultures and abilities by appealing to the universal human need for musical expression."

After taking the position of executive director in 1982, Hirsch became aware that, given the changing demographics of Chicago at that time, specifically in the Latino and African American communities, expanding his marketing efforts would be essential to the school's growth. He was also aware that many arts organizations were using outreach to get involved with communities of color, and that the bulk of this effort was underwritten by grants. In his model, he used consistent marketing tools and long-range thinking to expand his audience. He also made a twenty-five-year commitment to accomplishing this goal.

Among the steps undertaken by his institution were targeted programming for Latino communities, including bilingual marketing materials; ads in local Spanish media; and flyer distribution in traditionally underserved neighborhoods. Hirsch created a community outreach department and developed community ambassadors to build contacts, share dialogue and make recommendations for programs. Hirsch notes an important lesson he learned: "Executing a diversity plan in one community does not always translate exactly to every other target community. The principles of sensitivity, respect, open-mindedness and risk-taking are fundamental to audience development. Having someone on staff who is permanently responsible for diversity is a necessity—it helps to institutionalize the effort and keep all staff sensitized to this commitment."

It's important to have not only a dream, but also a *plan*. I have worked with arts organizations who were eager to expand their audiences but had no mission or sense of investment in the process. Ultimately, their efforts never took root and were, in fact, wasted, because although the potential audience was there, the institutional resources were never committed to the effort.

Your goal is to welcome these new audiences into your institution. Your job is to discover how and when to make this happen. It is not simply an acquisition of new mailing lists or stuffing programs with flyers (although, as we will see, such steps are of critical importance). It is much broader than that. You want to make sure you have established goodwill that is based on sincerity, honesty and the ability to make whatever you've outlined a reality.

Audience development requires a strategic plan that is holistically integrated into the fabric of your arts institution. The strategic plan must be grounded in the history of the institution, as well as the history of the audiences you are seeking to attract. It must be based on an understanding of and a willing openness to multiple cultures. More important than "filling seats" or meeting "the bottom line," the purpose of executing a strategic audience development plan is to build a long-lasting foundation for your institution grounded in the very communities you are opening your doors to serve.

And why is the arts so important? I believe it is the only tool we have that successfully crosses ethnic and cultural barriers, bridges misunderstanding, erases social strife and celebrates diversity. I have learned from experience that when diverse groups of people come together and experience the arts as one, that not only are they enriched by the experience, they also develop an appreciation for our shared humanity. Making the arts accessible to as broad an audience as possible helps us build a better society.

Those of us currently engaged in the effort to open the doors of our institutions to every segment of our community; those of us working to create an environment where people can support, enjoy and learn from the arts; and those of us fighting to maintain and grow the bottom line for our arts institutions have an arduous but essential, and even noble, mission.

Chapter 2

UNDERSTANDING THE LANGUAGE AND HISTORY OF AUDIENCE DEVELOPMENT

> The essence of art is its communication with the audience member. Therefore, arts organizations must shift their focus to enable, expand and enhance this communication. They must shift from a pure product focus to one that balances the artistic decision-making process with audience needs and preferences.
>
> —JOANNE SCHEFF AND PHILIP KOTLER
> *"Crisis in the Arts: The Marketing Response"*

To ensure we share the same understanding of the terminology used in the field of audience development, I want to spend some time discussing the terms that will be used continuously throughout this book.

In my twenty-four years of experience, I have heard a lot of definitions of and justifications for audience development work. Some institutions think of it as a means of "putting butts in the seats." Others think its purpose is to fulfill a grant requirement. It has been viewed as a tool for reaching a specific numeric goal so that diverse audiences can be quantified and touted at the next board meeting. It has been used to target audiences for an ethnic-specific play. I've even heard of audience development efforts being used to salvage institutions that are falling apart. All of these purposes are shortsighted, and their results short-term and ultimately ineffective. Why? Because there is little substance at the foundation of these efforts. They lack vision and strategy for implementation.

I define audience development as the cultivation and growth of long-term relationships, firmly rooted in a philosophical foundation that recognizes and embraces the distinctions of race, age, sexual orientation, physical disability, geography and class. Audience development is also the process of engaging, educating and motivating diverse communities to participate in a creative, entertaining experience as an important *partner* in the design and execution of the arts. Many institutions have been concerned that audience development efforts will somehow compromise or denigrate the integrity of the creative work being presented. But rather than compromise the artistic integrity, stretching beyond traditional boundaries and comfort zones requires that an organization strive for an even higher standard of excellence.

In the book *Audience Development: A Planning Toolbox for Partners* (Association of Performing Arts Presenters, Washington, D.C., 1994), Romalyn Eisenstark Tilghman notes the following objectives for work in this arena:

- To include adult arts education programs as a way to instill an understanding of and a commitment to the arts and the role of the artists
- To include projects that take place in connection with extended artists' residencies that involve the community in meaningful ways

- To attract new audiences who have not attended arts events in the past
- To develop culturally diverse or culturally specific audiences
- To deepen existing audiences' understanding of the arts
- To provide opportunities for audience participation in the arts.

Audience development is a specialized form of marketing that requires more than just the mastery of traditional marketing techniques, such as direct mail, series subscription drives, membership drives or advertising and press campaigns. Audience development is the merging of marketing techniques with relationship-building skills, because in order to have a lasting impact on your prospective audience, the relationship must be both personal *and* institutional. Your mission is to make a connection with your audiences' hearts by demonstrating the value of incorporating the arts into their lives. Once that connection is made, the idea of experiencing and supporting the arts and culture becomes organic, enabling the establishment of a long-term and loyal relationship. I refer to this type of action as "soft power."

Joseph Nye, Jr., former Dean of the Kennedy School of Government at Harvard University, coined the term "soft power" in the late 1980s. He used it to define the ability to attract and persuade, as opposed to a country's military or economic might. In the early 1990s a Japanese scholar and philosopher named Daisaku Ikeda further elaborated on this concept in a speech at Harvard University. He described the process of encouraging people to adopt or change their behavior based on inner motivation rather than through forceful dogma. What is the trigger for that inner motivation? The building of consensus and understanding among people through personal interaction and dialogue. That is the core of audience development work—building a consensus and understanding among people through personal interaction, dialogue *and* participation in the arts. Real audience development work is labor-intensive; it requires that *you* get in the trenches. A long-term process by nature, it also requires sensitivity, tenacity, persistence and courage.

Because audience development is also a collaborative process, the other key component is "internal" marketing. Why? If your audience development efforts are to be successful, every executive in your organization, every member of your board of directors, every department in your organization—from the person who answers the telephone to the person who collects the tickets at the door—must understand and support the initiative. Audience development is proactive (not reactive), socially responsible, internal and external marketing.

Audience development and "outreach" are not the same. Outreach entails an organization's making contacts and opening its doors. Audience development, on the other hand, is about making contacts, going into the communities you are trying to reach, engaging them in dialogue or activities related to the arts and your institution's activities, forming partnerships, and creating doors where none existed before.

The creation of those doors is what I will refer to throughout this book as "points of entry." The approach to effectively diversifying audiences must be fluid, an approach that allows the audience entry to the work, without the expectation that all audiences will respond in the same way. For example, when engaging in audience development work, you should not have the expectation that everyone you approach will be willing to pay for a ticket. Your potential audience may be more comfortable, certainly initially, with the opportunity to *sample* the work in some way. Your challenge is to create the door, the point of entry that will allow them access to the work, through the creative use of space, productions and resources.

One of the most critical aspects of audience development work, and the most sensitive, is the issue of race. To effectively create points of entry, you must understand your target audience. I'd like to spend some time discussing the historical issues that can (and will) impact any audience initiatives your institution may launch. The purpose of this discussion is not to create guilt, but rather to help develop an understanding of the facts.

Andrew Hacker, in his book *Two Nations* (Ballantine Books, New York, 1992), notes:

The significance of racism lies in the way it consigns certain human beings to the margins of society, if not painful lives and early deaths. In the United States, racism takes its highest toll on blacks. No white person can claim to have suffered in such ways because of ideas that may be held about them by some black citizens . . .

What is it, then, that makes white Americans unwilling to risk having black neighbors? To the minds of most Americans, the mere presence of black people is associated with a high incidence of crime, residential deterioration and lower educational attainment . . .

What we have come to call the media looms large in the lives of almost all Americans. Television and films, newspapers and magazines, books and advertising, all serve as windows on a wider world, providing real and fantasized images of the human experience.

Our media continues to perpetuate one-dimensional ethnic character stereotypes. Although the artistic community traditionally has been believed to be a bastion of liberalism, it cannot escape the larger social context in which art and culture exist in the United States today. Despite the increased numbers of minority-focused artistic ventures, most of which continue to struggle financially, whites primarily decide which people, plays, productions, concerts, films, etc., will be underwritten, produced or mounted and receive "mainstream exposure." In addition, the work of artists of color must past the stringent test of having "broad-based" appeal; otherwise the work may not be supported by the larger institutions. It is a test that is not applied to white artists.

What impact has this had on the artistic product? There have been times when mainstream white audiences have lauded the originality of artists of color, performers, musicians and athletes. But, in the end, the product that achieves the greatest commercial success is often the product that adapts to white sensibilities. A classic example of this is jazz, a true African American art form that has throughout history achieved popular success when played by white artists.

This cultural paradigm of exclusionary practices and co-opting of art has a long and stained history as old as slavery and segregation. America's history of racism has included the systematic exclusion of African Americans from popular entertainment—both in the degrading portrayals of blacks in every form of public amusement and in the policies of segregation. What was objectionable was not the conduct of blacks, but their mere presence. According to David Nasaw, in his book, *Going Out: The Rise and Fall of Public Amusements* (Harvard University Press, Cambridge, 1999), in the early nineteenth century, blacks were restricted to separate sections of the theatre, no matter how educated or wealthy they were, a practice that carried over into the twentieth century. They were assigned to a section only accessible from a back entrance off a dark alley—always the worst seats in the house, the upper balcony or gallery. Not only was the section never cleaned, blacks were forced to share it with prostitutes.

Minstrel shows were the first purported introduction of "black culture" to white audiences. However, the shows were not true interpretations of that culture, but rather humiliating parodies of southern blacks by whites, performed by white actors in blackface. In her book *Terrible Honesty* (Noonday Press, New York, 1996), renowned social and cultural historian Ann Douglas writes of the continued reverberations of the minstrel show's impact:

> Minstrelsy was racism in action: the expropriation and distortion of black culture for white purposes and profits. Minstrelsy put the fooling techniques of black culture . . . developed in the days of slavery, at the heart of American entertainment: blacks imitating and fooling whites, whites imitating and stealing from blacks . . . this is American popular culture.

This is *still* American popular culture, and the foundation for the differences between black (as well as other audiences of color) and white experiences with art and culture. This also partly explains the difficulties in getting audiences of color to explore white-produced entertainment, and the perception by people of color that white institutions do not respect their artistic talents or cultural needs.

Nasaw stresses that it wasn't until the civil rights movement of the 1950s and 1960s that there was an opening of doors to black audiences. It began with baseball, which was desegregated in 1947 (seven years before the desegregation of the public education system in 1954). Then amusement park owners began opening their doors to blacks as a result of insurmountable pressure from civil rights activists and legal authorities. However, in the '60s, using the pretenses of "unsafe subways and buses, problems with teenage hoodlums and inadequate parking," the owners circumvented the law by moving their amusement parks out of the urban areas, where they believed white visitors would now be discouraged from attending because of the growing influx of black patrons. Some white patrons stayed away from the parks merely because they were desegregated. As a former marketing director of Ohio's Cedar Point amusement park (now the largest such park in the world) was quoted as saying in Nasaw's book: "Many traditional patrons of the country's amusement parks did not feel comfortable sharing their amusement park experience with minorities."

According to Judith A. Adams, author of *The American Amusement Park Industry* (Twayne Publications, Boston, 1991), a comprehensive history of American amusement parks, the decision to build the new theme parks outside the cities was far from coincidental:

> Disneyland's location beyond the Los Angeles urban area, with no mass transit connections to the city, isolated it from the poorer elements of the urban population. Thus predominately middle- and upper-class clientele was ensured. Other theme parks have since copied.

Dr. Cornel West, in his book *Race Matters* (Beacon Press, Boston, 1993), raises another point:

> The common denominator of views on race is that people still see black people as a problem people . . . We confine discussions about race in America to the "problems" black

people pose for whites rather than consider what this way of viewing black people reveals about us as a nation . . . This framework encourages liberals to relieve their guilty consciences by supporting public funds directed at "the problems" . . . Hence for liberals, black people are to be "included" and "integrated" into "our" society and culture, while for conservatives they are to be "well-behaved" and "worthy of acceptance" by "our" way of life. Both fail to see that the presence and predicaments of black people are neither additions to nor defections from American life, but rather constitutive elements of that life.

The goal of audience development is not to *fix* the so-called "black problem." Neither is it about rescuing a forgotten, neglected or to-be-pitied group of people. With regard to ethnicity, the goal of audience development is to bridge the gap created by the systematic exclusion of people of color from art and culture. The history of exclusionary practices in the entertainment industry, coupled with the ongoing racist portrayal of communities of color in television programming and news media broadcasts, makes it clear that, in addition to our *desire* to open the doors of our institutions to diverse communities, it is of critical importance that audience development marketers also understand all the aspects of our nation's history of engagement with arts and culture. Once we have that understanding, we can cultivate the empathy and compassion necessary to develop, create and implement meaningful programs that serve as bridges to cross the divide.

Audience development also addresses America's history of disregard for the elderly and infatuation with youth. (The latter category, though highly sought after, does not voluntarily attend performances and exhibitions in great numbers.) The intensity and severity of these factors, as well as our nation's views on race and age, have had a long-term impact on the development of emerging audiences and on the ability of communities of color to embrace the arts.

The concept of a diverse audience can also be governed by location. In the farmlands—Appalachia and the Deep South, for example—motivating audiences to attend a cultural production in the city, rather than in their immediate community, is a form of diversification. Efforts to engage these audiences must also incorporate their special needs, such as transportation. It may, for instance, require making the cultural product mobile or transportable so that it can be accessed in rural areas. The circus, a traveling entertainment designed for mass audiences, provides one of the best laboratories in which to study the concept of unifying rural and urban audiences. Traditionally, neither class nor race has been problematic here—the circus appeals to everyone, it is promoted in all neighborhoods and carries an affordable ticket price.

In New York, geographical diversity has an economic undercurrent divided between its uptown and downtown neighborhoods, and between Manhattan and its surrounding boroughs. Many downtown arts organizations have launched intense efforts to engage traditional uptown theatregoers to explore downtown theatres, galleries and performance art spaces. The issue here is not one of developing an appreciation for the art form, but rather encouraging an already seasoned audience to extend its geographic comfort zone.

According to Scheff and Kotler ("Crisis in the Arts . . ." *California Management Review*, Fall 1996), the challenge is for arts managers and artists to reevaluate their attitudes about audiences:

> Arts organizations must be responsible to the needs of their audiences. Each and every current and potential arts patron—including single ticket buyers—should be respected, listened to, appreciated, and then when possible, nurtured into higher levels of commitment. If arts organizations do not respect and meet the public's changing needs as to how the product is offered, there will be an ever-diminishing audience to share in the artistic experiment.

Scheff and Kotler add that the purpose of an arts organization is to expose an artist and his or her message to the widest possible audience, rather than to produce the artist and the message that the largest audience demands.

They suggest that arts managers face three major challenges today. First, they must help create the understanding that art needs to be an integral part of people's everyday lives. Second, the arts organizations' management and marketing teams must be professional and strategic, as well as open to developing initiatives that will be the most responsive to the needs and interests of their public. Finally, arts organizations must be sensitive and responsive to the political and social trends that have an impact on their efforts.

The trend in public funding is a case in point. In the '60s and '70s, audiences attended performing arts events in record numbers. The National Endowment for the Arts, established in 1965, provided financial support for many new arts programs and performances. In the '80s, the focus shifted to commercial economic development: more emphasis was placed on the importance of acquiring assets and raising money, lessening the emphasis on the performing arts themselves. The advent of the '90s brought a severe cutback in government funding for the arts, and arts organizations were forced to look to the private sector for support. But the downsizing at many corporations meant cutbacks in their support of the arts as well. Ticket prices increased, often forcing individual consumers to choose between the luxury of going to the theatre and their necessities. The severe financial climate, coupled with increased competition from the video and movie industries, reduced attendance to performing arts events.

The '90s also saw some positive shifts in the field of audience development. In 1997, the Theatre Development Fund and The League of American Theatres and Producers released the first benchmark study of the New York theatre audience, including Broadway and Off-Broadway productions. The study found that younger theatregoers are more ethnically diverse than their elders. Asian American, Hispanic American and African American theatregoers accounted for 12.9% of the total Broadway audience and 10.9% of the total Off-Broadway audience. In the 18–24-year range, Asian American, Hispanic American and African American theatregoers represented 20% of the Broadway audience and 25.4% of the Off-Broadway audience. Overall, the survey found that the audience for Broadway was younger than it had been in 1991. In 1997, 41.8% of theatregoers were under 35, a 7% increase from 1991. The student population in the audience grew 4%, while the under-18 age group grew 7%. Because of technological advances, especially the internet, our younger generation has a greater exposure to diverse cultures, and is in turn more open to difference— to a difference in cultures, art, music, fashion, politics, etc. This openness presents us with a great opportunity for audience growth.

The National Endowment for the Arts' 1997 survey of public participation in the arts reinforced the TDF/LATP statistical analysis by showing that the number of people of color engaging in the arts was growing. For example, non-ballet dance audiences have higher proportional representations of Latinos, African Americans and Asians than Caucasians, when compared to the total population. Classical music concerts, operas, non-musical plays and art museums all have a higher percentage of Asian representation as well. These figures show that there is a growing ethnic audience attending arts performances.

These statistics suggest that we have an opportunity to build a diverse and young audience, if we choose to proactively engage in strategically planned, fully integrated audience development.

Chapter 3

TEN TOOLS FOR
BUILDING AUDIENCES

> If we want to influence or encourage people, we
> have to deeply understand them, not just by
> using listening techniques, but by our example,
> our actual conduct. This involves the shift from
> listening with the intent to reply, to listening to
> really understand.
>
> —STEPHEN R. COVEY
> *The 7 Habits of Highly Effective People*

Earlier I defined a major component of audience development as the merging of marketing techniques with relationship-building skills. I believe the key to building long-term relationships is the mastery of an art we all possess but don't always utilize: the art of listening.

Stephen R. Covey, author of *The 7 Habits of Highly Effective People* (Simon and Schuster, New York, 1989), says listening is more important than asking questions, and he offers three important principles related to this highly necessary skill: look directly at the person who is speaking, learn to listen with everything you've got, and forget yourself completely. Why is this important? Successful audience development requires that we talk to our potential audience, hear what they have to say, and incorporate their ideas into the work of our institutions. Rather than project what we *think* other people need or want, or project our intentions onto the behavior of others, Covey says, we need to *understand* them as individuals. In other words, we don't need to project any cultural, social or historical biographies onto the way we look at individuals. Yes, those issues have influence, but they don't represent the totality of the cultural experience of the diverse groups of communities we are seeking to reach.

I was deeply inspired by Monty Roberts's book *The Man Who Listens to Horses* (Random House, New York, 1997). Roberts explains that his ability to listen to horses, to read their signs and respond to their needs, grew out of his practice of patience, humility and open-mindedness. Noting that horses can understand everything said to them and that they can tell a lot about a person through observation, Roberts created a process called "join-up," in which he engages in communication with the horse and builds trust by allowing himself to be vulnerable. Consequently, Roberts says, the horse voluntarily decides to work with him in his endeavors. This philosophy of listening is rooted in a belief that the utmost respect should be extended to *all* living beings. He continues:

> For centuries humans have said to horses, "You do what I tell you or I'll hurt you." Humans still say that to each other, still threaten and force and intimidate. I am convinced that my discoveries with horses also have value in the workplace, in the educational and penal systems, in the raising of children. At heart I am saying that no one has the right to say "you must" to anyone. Trust has to be won between people and the organization.

I believe the way to create and build that trust is by implementing what I call the Ten Tools for Building Audiences. They are:

— 1. —

Investment

— 2. —

Commitment

— 3. —

Research

— 4. —

Educating Your Artists and Audiences

— 5. —

Review and Analysis

— 6. —

Follow-up

— 7. —

Partnership

— 8. —

Building the Bridge/Extending the Invitation

— 9. —

Creating Value

— 10. —

Appreciation

I will explain each of these terms in detail, and, in Chapters 4 and 5, I will show how the application of these Ten Tools helped turn around the efforts of two renowned arts institutions: Dance Theatre of Harlem and The Joseph Papp Public Theater/New York Shakespeare Festival.

1. Investment: Building Your Resources for the Future

To invest means to put in the time and effort for a future return. Income and profit will ultimately be reflected in sales, but the act of participating in audience development is first and foremost an investment in the future, not a short-term boost in box-office receipts. This critical point needs to be embraced by every member of your organization, from the board of directors and executive staff to the ushers and ticket-sellers. Do not expect results tomorrow, next week or even next month. You are informing a new constituency about your product, you are striving to develop relationships, and you are developing ways for these future arts consumers to become comfortable with accessing what it is you have to offer. This takes time.

Audience development is a long-term, labor-intensive process that also requires a sense of vision and purpose. It requires an understanding of all the complexities and nuances of your institution's art form, so that you may be as creative as possible in the implementation of your initiatives. This means investing time in getting to know your institution from top to bottom—what it stands for and where it's going. Bigger budgets and bigger staffs would be nice, but you need to be realistic. You will be responsible for proving that whatever investment is made will yield benefits for your institution. Therefore, you will be challenged to find ways to work with minimal resources. But remember: It can be done.

Just remember that by broadening the reach of your institution, you are planting seeds for its future. It's like putting money in a 401(k) plan, rather than playing the stock market.

2. Commitment: The Long Haul . . . Refusing to Turn Back

Commitment to this process is essential, particularly when working with a small budget and minimal resources (staff, time and product). You must also be creative, tenacious and focused. A passion for audience development is imperative. This work requires a commitment to attaining a result regardless of the long journey ahead: One cannot give up on efforts when change doesn't happen right away, or lose faith in a community that lacks the ability to respond at the start. The results will happen—with your commitment of time and passion. This means going beyond the normal workday. It means making yourself available to your constituents. It means extending you life to support *their* goals, recognizing that this is an opportunity to build trust. It means serving on boards and joining community organizations in order to create mutual support.

3. Research: Who Is the Audience?

Research is the most important component of audience development, and it never stops. Two kinds of research are necessary: the quantitative research tells you the numbers and percentage of ticket buyers and provides statistics on other buying habits; the qualitative research speaks to how and why a particular audience member responds to a cultural product, it examines behavior but does not provide projectable numbers. When you engage in qualitative research, it is important to consider how you ask the questions *and* how you interpret the answers. Ask your questions from a place of sincerity, genuine interest and compassion. There is no "wrong" answer, no need for guilt or recrimination.

When is the right time to embark on this quest? When you have a solid understanding of the art you represent and a vision of what you want to accomplish. When you know the questions to ask: Why haven't you been coming? What do you like? What is the best time to present programs? Where do you like to hang out?

Who are the key people to include in this dialogue? It is important to understand the buying habits of the audiences you are trying to reach. Ethnic, age, class and geographical distinctions play a major role in ticket-buying behavior. Sources to assist you in finding your target groups include national directories of ethnic-specific organizations, teen and youth programs, and local phone and internet directories. You may even form a think tank to better understand your goals and obstacles, and create solutions based on a collective understanding of the issues. But sometimes one key person in a community is the only ambassador you need.

After you have done your research, there is an expectation that something will happen. In *The 7 Habits of Highly Effective People*, Covey talks about personal integrity. Ultimately, your word is all you have. It is also important that you treat everyone with the same set of principles. As you work with different communities, it is important not to adopt different sets of behaviors from one group to the other. This type of behavior will undermine your sincerity and suggest that your motivation is agenda-based or perhaps biased.

4. Educating Your Artists and Audiences: Demystifying the Art Product

Audience development means educating not only your audiences but also the artists whose work is ultimately the foundation on which the initiative rests. You have to take on the role of educators, creating systems that inform your artists and audience about your vision and that build support based on shared interests.

To educate artists means to share with them the vision of your institution so they become aware of the larger goal beyond the creation of their own projects. You must make them understand that the initiative is greater than a single brilliant performance, that the audience is a *necessary* component of their creative process, that it is crucial to collectively make this artistic experience as inclusive as possible. If the artists remain uninformed, you will lose out on a vital component of audience development: artist interaction. Let them know about your efforts to cultivate a broader-based audience. This will serve you well when it is time to do promotional activities and hold public discussions, book/poster signings, etc. I am *not* suggesting that artists become marketers, I am suggesting that artists bring a richness to the big picture. Take advantage of that.

To educate the audience also requires that you share your vision with them. This requires creativity and the integration of the cultural nuances of the communities you are seeking to reach. Audiences need to understand what it is they're being encouraged to see in *advance* of the performance. Be open to suggestions and a new way of building your audiences. Just because your institution has been around for years doesn't mean that the people living across the street have ever been inside. They may not know what you have to offer—but most likely they have not been invited.

Educating your audience means helping them understand the importance of connecting their lives to your product. How do you educate them? You have many options (videos, DVDs, the internet, blogs and podcasts are just the tip of the iceberg). Be innovative. And don't forget your most important tool—people.

5. Review and Analysis: Unravel the Data

Once you've completed your research, the next step is review and analysis. What type of information do you have? What do you do with it? How can you integrate what you've learned into your existing programming? What opportunities can you create internally to manifest these plans?

The review and analysis phase reveals the importance of internal support in the creation of programs and events (discounts, free performances, for example), and makes clear how you may utilize other internal resources to attract a broader audience. You may not have all the solutions, but by engaging in a dialogue with the creative staff as well as your marketing and public relations staff, you can craft a plan of action *together* that is responsive yet not a drain on the resources of your institution. Keeping your bottom line in mind, what is the expectation? Is it a percentage increase in box-office income? Is it a particular number of new projects? Are results expected now, or can they evolve over time? To set your goals clearly, you must first *define them.*

In addition to your research, be sure to review and analyze your current strategies. Are they working? Why or why not?

6. Follow-up: Keeping Your Promise

After you've conducted your research and assessed the data, give it legs! Discuss internally what you can do—what steps can you take to signal to your communities: "I hear you," "Let's try this" or "What do you think?" Then go back to the people with whom you met to discuss your ideas. If nothing happens as a result of the time and effort that all parties have made in the process, your work will have been a waste of time, and your organization will lose its credibility and respect. There must be some measurable accomplishment; otherwise your potential new constituency will lose faith in you and your institution.

7. Partnership: Building Your Team

If you want to create partnerships based on shared benefits and mutual respect, then you must be as diverse in your programming as you want your audience to be. This can be difficult. Many artistic directors, producers and presenters have a certain mindset about the type of cultural product they want to bring to their audiences. They are more comfortable and familiar with traditional art and culture. However, we're talking about expanding the base of our institutions to embrace non-traditional consumers. If you ask, this new audience can and will tell you what it likes. Ideal programming represents a cultural product for new audiences *in addition* to traditional offerings.

Partnership is the building block of all relationships. Don't be afraid to share. This does not mean handing over the reins of artistic control or management. It means sharing ideas and concepts and being willing to listen wholeheartedly. Collaborate with communities so that they embrace the entire institution, not just a single production. This is the true spirit of "building an audience." It is a combination of designing programs, initiating projects, exposing new audiences and, together, setting goals that are realistic.

8. Building the Bridge/Extending the Invitation:
Crafting the Overall Experience

Suppose you hear about a party being held every week, but you are not invited. Judging by the buzz around town, this party is the hip place to be, so even though you are not given a formal invitation, you decide to go. When you get there, although it is exciting, you feel awkward, self-conscious. You wonder whether the hosts are whispering about why you are there. You wonder if other guests know you weren't invited. No one speaks to you or acknowledges your presence. Finally, you get the hint. You leave. You decide you'll never go back. Eventually you lose interest in the party, and then finally you don't even remember that the weekly party is going on.

For audiences who feel excluded from arts institutions (whether the exclusion is conscious or unconscious) the experience is the same: there is a party—an art opening, a dance concert, a theatre production—and they were not invited. It doesn't matter that display advertisements appeared in the *New York Times*, *Los Angeles Times* or *Chicago Tribune*, or that banner ads were placed on the internet or radio spots broadcast on the all-news radio stations. Your nontraditional audience is still not responding. The question is, why?

In most instances, your research should inform you. But the answer actually depends upon the culture of the particular group you are targeting. How can you encourage your guests to leave their houses and come to a party at yours? You need to determine: Who extends the invitation? What does it look like? What is its form? Are there any caveats? How long is the invitation for? These questions are very important. The answers may be found by considering one of the cornerstones of marketing: "Know your audience." The marketing strategy may require community-based partnerships, targeted programming, free events, group sales or the creation of events that have a social component and allow groups to participate more easily.

Language, graphic design and color can also impact whether the invitation is successful. How and when you choose to advertise is just as important as the look and design. Explore local resources, such as community papers, church newsletters, fraternity newsletters and professional associations; send email blasts to local social groups and reading groups. In many instances, this grassroots method proves a much more effective invitation than the expensive display ads placed in your daily newspaper.

Just as important as your targeted outreach, is the quality of the experience you provide your new guests. Because first impressions can make or break you, the welcome is extremely important. Who will be there to greet your new friends? Do they understand why this is important? How are they dressed? Are they warm and friendly? Is there a welcome mat at the door? Making audience development an institutional vision is a critical component of its long-term success.

9. Creating Value: Creative Definitions

Audience development is not charity work. It is making arts and culture accessible to everyone. We are not building audiences simply to increase earned income. Creating value is not always reflected dollar-for-dollar in a changed bottom line. Initially the effort is to open the doors of your institution to diverse audiences and collaborate on programs they want to see. That is what will *keep* the doors open.

Be aware that you cannot create value just by giving away free tickets. Recipients feel no loyalty to an institution merely because it distributes complimentary admission. Without a foundation based on relationships or an understanding of why discount or complimentary tickets are available, this process is nonproductive. I believe everyone should pay *something*. If you provide complimentary tickets, it should always be with the understanding that it is being done as an investment in your ongoing relationship, that together you are building the strength of the institution. Your institution should receive something back as well. You do not want to send a message that audience development means: "I'm helping the underserved by giving out these free tickets." What value is created by that gesture? None. You've given away twenty tickets (and given the recipients the option *not* to use them) because there was no collaboration or dialogue about the relationship you are attempting to establish. Creating value means developing a sense of purpose for the institution and helping the audience feel a sense of responsibility to that relationship. For example, students who receive free tickets may be asked to write a paper about the production in conjunction with the curriculum for their class.

10. Appreciation: "Thank You!" Is the World's Most Powerful Phrase

Henry James wrote:

Three things in life are important: The first is to be kind. The second is to be kind. The third is to be kind.

Success comes down to the little things we do. Terrie Williams, in her book with Joe Cooney, *The Personal Touch* (Warner Books, New York, 1994), offers several illustrations of how acknowledging people's efforts has enabled her to maintain one of the most successful public relations firms in the country. What can we learn from Henry James and Terrie Williams?

In your effort to build new audiences, expressing appreciation is critical. When one is magnanimous, when there is a true generosity of spirit, this opens the door for a flow of mutual respect and a willingness from your constituency to support your efforts. Marketers and producers need to appreciate the efforts made by audience members to embrace the work; artists need to appreciate the efforts of marketers to convey the essence of their work to audiences; and audiences need to be made to appreciate the efforts of both. Be sure to send thank-you notes to each person who does something to help your effort—no matter how small—participating in a telephone conversation, furnishing a name or a list, sharing an idea, attending your event or providing a service.

Using these Ten Tools makes a difference in your organization. But, if you cannot implement all ten, you may be able to implement eight, five or three. Develop a plan and get started. It all begins with taking the first step.

There is a modern-day adage popularized by the film *Field of Dreams* that, with modification, applies to audience development work:

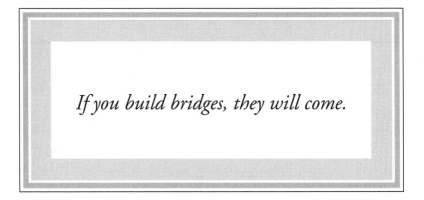

If you build bridges, they will come.

Chapter 4

CREATING THE MAGIC: DANCE THEATRE OF HARLEM

The heart is most important of all. In his classic, *The Little Prince*, Antoine de Saint-Exupéry writes: "It is only with the heart that we see rightly; what is essential is invisible to the eye."

—DAISAKU IKEDA
PRESIDENT, SOKA GAKKAI INTERNATIONAL–USA

My own love affair with the arts began in Chicago during the 1960s. It started when I was five years old, with dance. My mother drove my twin sister and me to ballet classes every week for five years. We also took piano and baton-twirling lessons. At age thirteen, my sister and I took African dance lessons, and we began performing with the Julian Swain Inner City Dance Theatre, then later with Najwa Dance Corps, a company that grew out of Julian's. Then, when I was in high school, an attorney visited our class as part of a career-day event. That same night I told my mother I wanted to become a lawyer. Nonetheless, I continued taking dance classes throughout high school and college. While in law school at Howard University, I discovered a ballet teacher, Diane Petty, who was as crazy as I was about dance. Her classes were held at seven A.M. on weekdays, and no matter how much studying I had to do, I began every single day by dancing.

After graduating from law school in 1980, I got married and moved to New York, where I decided to practice law. But I discovered that I was not able to stay away from working in the arts. Less than a year after I arrived, a colleague told me about the Thelma Hill Performing Arts Center, which is dedicated to the professional development of dancers and choreographers of color. The center was located across the street from Brooklyn's Family Court, where I worked as assistant corporation counsel, prosecuting juveniles and handling child support cases. She said the facility presented great music and dance concerts, featuring local artists. I stopped by on my lunch hour one day and introduced myself to Larry Phillips, who was running the center alone. It was obvious to me during our conversation that he needed help, so I volunteered to assist him. He welcomed my efforts, despite my obvious inexperience. I used my lunch hour to study marketing, fund-raising and public relations so that I could develop collateral materials, such as media kits and brochures. I looked through telephone directories to compile lists of churches and other organizations that could be targeted with our materials. I developed relationships with reporters and editors at black newspapers, and coverage of the center began to increase. I taught myself proposal writing, although my first attempt was disastrous—I couldn't reconcile the budget and was over-confident about my ability to prepare the proposal in the traditional manner. It was late and ill-prepared, and, as a result, the center did not receive the requested amount. But a valuable lesson was learned.

The time I spent developing and polishing my skills to help the center was intellectually stimulating and emotionally satisfying, and it re-ignited my passion for dance. I began to see the results of my efforts—more people began to fill the house whenever the center sponsored or produced a performance. It took less than a year for me to realize that I no longer wanted to be just a volunteer; I decided to resign my position at family court. Larry applied for and received a grant to pay me a modest salary to work part-time, thus beginning my career as an arts administrator. It was during my tenure at the Thelma Hill Performing Arts Center that my ideas for creating nontraditional audience outreach programs first were launched.

In 1984, after working at the center a few years, I was eager for an opportunity to further expand my skills and learn more from other arts organizations. I sent a letter to Arthur Mitchell, Co-Founder (with Karel Shook) and Artistic Director of Dance Theatre of Harlem (DTH), one of the nation's premier classical ballet companies. DTH was—and is—a multicultural company, predominantly comprised of African Americans. Serendipitously, my letter arrived on the day DTH's audience development coordinator resigned. It was four weeks before the company was scheduled to open a month-long run at New York's City Center, where it was going to premiere a new version of the classical ballet *Giselle*, choreographed by Mr. Mitchell, renamed *Creole Giselle* and set in the Louisiana bayous. The company's staff and board anticipated that the production might generate some controversy, and they wanted to be sure that it did not adversely affect ticket sales. Arthur Mitchell hired me immediately. He gave me only one charge—sell tickets.

Based on what I had learned while working at the Thelma Hill Performing Arts Center, I began making calls right away. There were times when my telephone calls were not returned and my efforts were rejected. I learned through trial and error. And I never gave in to setbacks—each experience was welcome, because it provided another brick in the foundation I was building for my audience development work. I contacted many of the groups I had cultivated with Larry Phillips and encouraged them to buy tickets. Within a month, I had established enough contacts and sold enough tickets to meet DTH's projections, and *Creole Giselle* was performed before packed houses at City Center.

A year and a half later, Mr. Mitchell made me his personal and administrative assistant. Not only did I get to observe firsthand all aspects of operating a ballet company, I also got to travel with DTH as it toured France, Italy, Spain, Brazil, Argentina, Venezuela and several countries in Africa. I learned a lot during these DTH tours, especially in the area of marketing, and I wanted the opportunity to implement my experience in audience development, group sales and special events. So Mr. Mitchell made me marketing associate, and a few years later I became director of marketing.

Breaking Through the Barriers

During a discussion about our upcoming 1988 season, Mr. Mitchell and I talked about the lack of attendance by African Americans at DTH performances outside New York City, where we had developed a strong reputation and loyal following among people of color.

"I don't understand it," he said. "Where are all the black people?" It was particularly surprising because DTH was touring Detroit, St. Louis and Chicago, cities that had fairly sizeable African American populations. The issue for Mr. Mitchell was not financial—the company's performances were selling out. He became determined to break through the barriers (the same barriers that had originally led him to establish DTH in 1969) that were keeping people of color away from the company's performances.

As we planned our national tour, we began questioning several of our presenters about the marketing strategies they used to attract African Americans to DTH performances. To our surprise, we learned that, although they were sincere in their intentions, they had developed no specific plan or special marketing materials to reach those audiences. We realized that if the situation were to change, we would have to get involved directly. Our first opportunity came later that year as we approached the 1989 season and DTH's twentieth anniversary.

While looking through file cabinets, I discovered something very special: archives of DTH photographs. The late Michael Scherker, then DTH's staff librarian, helped me sort through the trove of pictures I found: photos of classes, performances, open houses, tours and special guests who had attended performances over the decades and posed backstage with the dancers. I had an idea to present some of these in celebration of the anniversary. I asked Michael, "Wouldn't it be great if we could somehow exhibit these? At the Guggenheim, at the reception to launch the twentieth anniversary of the founding of the company? We could curate a photo exhibition documenting Dance Theatre of Harlem's history."

"We could invite some of the former dancers," he added.

"And honor them for helping DTH develop its world-renowned reputation," I concluded.

"It's a great idea, Donna, but how will we pay for it?"

Of course, there was no budget for such an exhibition. However, one of the greatest lessons that I've learned is based on the adage: "Leap and the net will appear." Once you develop an idea and create a plan, the necessary resources will somehow emerge to support the effort. I shared the photo exhibition idea with our development department and discovered that, coincidentally, one of the associates had already been talking to Kodak about corporate sponsorship of DTH. Although there had been no response to her efforts so far, she believed the exhibition might be something Kodak would support.

After a flurry of telephone calls and letters, a check for $5,000 arrived from Kodak. We selected 145 8 x 10 photos to include in the exhibit and solicited the support of DTH's alumni to help develop brief summaries that would accompany each picture. This turned out to be a great way to document the history of the company while making the alumni an integral part of the process.

We had the photos mounted in Brooklyn, and I went to Kodak's headquarters in Rochester, NY, to supervise the framing. Kodak also built sturdy, padded, wooden shipping crates that could withstand any travel conditions (this would come in handy for touring the exhibit). But we still needed a way to display them at the reception. I called various exhibition equipment and office supply stores around New York. When I explained that the exhibition saluting the alumni was part of the DTH twentieth anniversary reception at the Guggenheim, one of the stores loaned me sufficient free-standing panels to mount all 145 photographs in exchange for several tickets to a New York performance. This was a savings of almost

$800. From that experience I learned that when there is no budget, bartering tickets is a viable—and very lucrative—option.

I had one more obstacle: We needed money to purchase the adhesive backing necessary to affix the photos to the panels. I asked a board member, who gladly sent a check. We then began the process of cataloging the photographs for the exhibition. While working with my colleagues to label each photo, we realized the photographic exhibition could potentially have its own life as an educational tool in support of the company's tour. The photos captured important moments in history for African Americans and ballet. We could arrange the photos differently by time periods, ballets or choreography. With the crates Kodak had provided and the development of additional signage, we could ship the DTH Retrospective Photo Exhibit (as it was to become titled) to our tour sites in advance of DTH's engagements. Later, as the plan was refined and implemented, we asked each presenter to cover the shipping costs themselves. In some cases they could not accommodate all 145 photos, so we created mini-exhibits, some as small as twenty-five photos, that would still convey the sense of the company's history and its activities. Over the years, the photos were shown not only in theatres and art galleries, but also in libraries, boutiques, shopping malls and bookstores. They even were on display in the better dress department of Macy's in Washington, D.C., as part of DTH's Kennedy Center engagement. That same year, one of the principal dancers, Keith Saunders, pulled out all the photos of prima ballerina Virginia Johnson and created an exhibit honoring her twenty-year career with DTH, which was shown at Howard University's Blackburn Center. This event was an important point of entry into the young African American community.

Creating the Force for Change

In 1989, a scheduled weeklong engagement in Cleveland, Ohio, became the testing ground for new directions in our marketing and outreach, using not only our touring photo exhibition but also a new audience development task force. The marketing department of the Cleveland Ballet initially formed the task force, which was at first comprised of prominent local African American political, religious and civic leaders. Three months before our first performance, the task force began working with the marketing staff to shape the ballet's public relations and marketing campaign to specifically target the African American community. The group's goal was to encourage professional associations, arts organizations and media contacts to support the DTH performances, as well as to offer subsidized tickets to youth, religious and senior groups. The task force enthusiastically embraced its mission. It was these civic leaders who suggested, for example, that we hold a reception several weeks in advance of the opening to showcase the photo exhibition, allowing local audiences to learn more about DTH and its important place in African American culture and history. They believed that giving people the opportunity to attend a reception and view the photographs would spur ticket sales, and they were right. The company sold out its performances and, more important, the foundation was built for ongoing relationships between the African American community and the Cleveland Ballet.

I realized through the success of the photo exhibit that I could expand its benefits by videotaping the reception in Cleveland. The tape could then be used for booking, development work, and as a way to introduce the company to groups for possible advance ticket sales. I hired a local company (since I'm not a videographer) and worked as the director during the reception. I later wrote a script, supervised the editing of the tape and chose the music for the seven-minute video, which was narrated by DTH's prima ballerina, Virginia Johnson. The total cost of the production was only $700, and turned out to be money well spent.

Removing Barriers and Building Bridges

After a discussion with Mr. Mitchell about the success of the Cleveland campaign, I decided to build on what we had learned and establish a task force in advance of DTH performances whenever possible, using many of the strategies we developed in Cleveland. My assistant, Williann Middleton, and I began traveling to different tour cities to talk to African American community leaders about DTH.

At one of our early task force meetings on the West Coast, we were questioned about the relevance and purpose of DTH. We were challenged by the group's perception that ballet was a "white" art form, and therefore irrelevant to them. At that moment of confrontation, I realized that we had assumed that African Americans would automatically want to embrace DTH out of a sense of pride because we were a black company. I was insensitive to what many African Americans perceived as barriers to accessing ballet, such as the fact that none of the other major ballet companies at that time featured any African Americans as principal dancers. This was an invaluable lesson for me. I learned that if we want an audience to embrace our product, we must make sure they fully understand who we are and what we do. To be effective, we cannot assume that people will embrace us just because we are *artists*, or just because the company happens to be of the same ethnicity, religion, race, gender or sexual orientation as the potential audience. Personal histories as well as societal factors will always play major roles in determining whether we can develop relationships with diverse audiences. More importantly, I recognized that if I were going to win people over, my response to their challenge would have to be embracing, nondefensive and nonjudgmental.

To remove the barriers and build a bridge, we began a dialogue with the aim of educating this prospective audience about ballet, particularly its relationship to African American culture. Some of the things we discussed with them included the difficulties of mastering the art form and the years of study it requires. We also shared how Mr. Mitchell gave up his own successful career as a premier dancer with New York City Ballet to create DTH in 1969, the year following the assassination of the Reverend Dr. Martin Luther King, Jr. We explained his sense of mission—how he established DTH as a place where classically trained African American dancers could perform and polish their craft. We told them how Mr. Mitchell demanded that his dancers not only be excellent artists, but also intelligent and eloquent people. We shared his vision that DTH would become a cultural ambassador for the United States, traveling worldwide to showcase the exceptional and brilliant talents of the company while fighting bigotry and helping erase the perception that blacks could not perform ballet.

During the next year, as our outreach efforts intensified, we were better able to articulate DTH's mission and the work of the audience development task force to prospective participants. As the task force evolved, we determined its goals:

- To educate audiences about the value of supporting the arts as an educational tool that can encourage individuals to think critically and creatively, and to contribute positively to society.
- To educate audiences about the need to support the arts financially.
- To develop new audiences, including nontraditional audiences who had never attended a performance for various reasons, including financial need, lack of knowledge, lack of interest, intimidation or fear of not understanding the art form.
- To create partnerships among the theatre, the artists and local communities in support of all incoming programming, creating a sense of ownership, personal interest and commitment from the community to the arts organization.

From that point forward, working alone or with my assistant, I would arrive at our national presenting venues approximately three to six months in advance of each engagement to meet with the presenting organization and work with them to establish a local task force. Usually the presenting organization had one or two names of African American journalists or political, community or religious leaders whom we could call to get the ball rolling. We first needed to find co-chairs and/or honorary co-chairs who could help us to recruit other task force members. Once we had a list of names, we would get everybody together for a large kickoff meeting to organize subcommittees, which focused on public relations, fund-raising, education, special group sales, religious community outreach and business sponsorships.

Volunteers from the community who worked in those specific fields were sought to head the subcommittees—for example, a publicist would chair the public relations committee, a minister's wife would head the church committee, a teacher would head the education committee, and so on. In this way, the subcommittee chair could lend his or her expertise to the task force in order to develop creative outreach projects.

We learned fairly quickly that in order for the task force to be effective, the committee chairs had to be well organized and possess the ability to inspire and galvanize people to achieve the outlined short- and long-term objectives. The short-term objective, of course, was to sell tickets by setting up timelines and developing strategies to reach the financial and seat goals. The long-term objective was to educate prospective audiences about the value of investing in the arts in their communities and of forming mutually beneficial partnerships with the host institutions.

Ultimately, two factors contributed to the effectiveness of the audience development task force—our ability to get task force members to believe that they could, in fact, achieve their goals; and the willingness of the presenting organization to open itself up to feedback and input from the potential audiences we targeted. For those two things to happen, it was imperative that there always be open and honest communication among DTH staff, the presenting organization and participants in the task force.

After each kickoff meeting, I would spend the next two or three days in meetings, sometimes from ten A.M. to ten P.M., with task force members and the presenters. I had to help build the foundation for the task force, make sure that the presenters and the task force leaders were communicating effectively, and quickly troubleshoot any problems that might arise. The task force's committees, in addition to being clear about their objectives, had to have open relationships with the presenter and had to be able to continue their work once I returned to New York. I was always available by telephone, but the task force and the presenters performed the day-to-day work on the front lines. I performed these tasks in addition to handling the day-to-day responsibilities of marketing the company and working with our publicist, Ellen Zeisler, to position our efforts in the media.

DTH's use of audience development task forces fundamentally changed the way we reached out to our audiences, by not only getting them involved in our marketing efforts, but also allowing them to develop partnerships with the presenting organizations, which gave them a sense of ownership and mission. In a sense, DTH became the bridge that ultimately forged lasting relationships between presenting organizations and local communities. I would like to share a few specific examples with you.

During the 1989 season, DTH was booked by the University of Washington to perform in its 1,800-seat Meany Hall for one week. At that time, the African American population in Seattle was approximately 5%. Three months before the engagement, I flew to Seattle and set up meetings with many African American community leaders who were recommended to me by Meany Hall's marketing director. To promote the upcoming performances, we formed a local audience development task force of 250 people, chaired by Dr. Constance Rice, the wife of then-mayor Norman Rice. The task force, which was comprised of entrepreneurs, educators, leaders of professional organizations, ministers and artists, decided its focus would be recruiting businesses to participate, conducting education outreach and publicizing the performance. As a result of their activities (which included the successful pitching of stories about DTH's upcoming performance to local reporters), there was a 30% increase in ticket sales. When DTH arrived in Seattle, we organized a reception so that the university's task force could meet the dancers personally. The eloquence, intelligence and grace of the dancers so impressed the task force that its members decided to purchase 1,800 tickets for students in elementary through high school so that they could attend a free performance. Owners of local fast-food franchises took responsibility for this fund-raising effort, and in less than one week, $48,000 was collected to purchase the tickets. In addition, the Boeing Company donated buses to transport the children to the theatre, and the task force provided 100 volunteers to supervise the children once inside. So that more people could experience DTH, the Black Employee Association at Microsoft duplicated 200 copies of a segment about Mr. Mitchell and DTH that had aired on *60 Minutes*. The segment, narrated by Ed Bradley, highlighted DTH's school and a recent European tour. Those videos were distributed free and were shown in schools, libraries, churches, homes and community centers throughout Seattle.

Less than a month later, the task force in Sacramento, CA, and the local presenter, the University of California at Davis, provided a thousand tickets to DTH's lecture demonstration series for economically disadvantaged youth. UC Davis also formed a task force on its campus to inform and educate university students about DTH and encourage them to purchase tickets. This campaign resulted in a 15% increase in ticket sales over the previous year, plus the establishment of a new relationship between UC Davis and Sacramento's African American community.

My experiences in Seattle and Sacramento taught me that once arts administrators empower the community with the idea that anything is possible, the community's determination can make anything happen. These groups had never done work like this before. There were no proposals written and there was no budget. Nonetheless, all five of DTH's performances were sold out in Seattle, and we had tremendous audience growth in Sacramento. In addition, DTH recruited two of the Seattle task force members to join its own board of directors. I learned that audience development could be a powerful tool for fund-raising, especially in the wake of diminishing governmental and corporate support for the arts. Most importantly, I learned the value of asking the community to support its own.

Spotlight on Our Efforts

Our audience development efforts garnered both local and national attention. In December 1991, Barbara Ross, in *Black Enterprise* magazine, described how DTH's audience development campaigns reached out to "organizations that already have deep roots in the black community—churches, colleges, art galleries, single-parent groups—to attract audiences that can't be reached through traditional marketing and advertising. Relationships with national black organizations, such as the Links, Inc. and Jack and Jill of America, also helped promote awareness of DTH. The Washington, D.C., chapter of Jack and Jill sponsored an after-school reception at a local Macy's store, where area youngsters could meet the dancers and win tickets to DTH performances at the Kennedy Center. The event raised $2,300 for DTH."

ACE Magazine, a national arts publication, described how I went "into beauty parlors and retail stores pitching the benefits of being involved in the arts. In several cities, black-owned McDonald's franchises in predominately black communities were stuffing flyers into the bags, mounting posters and creating tray fillers. In Harlem, the McDonald's on West 125th Street showed video clips of DTH in its store. Aside from the benefits of increased audience support, the outreach efforts helped fulfill Arthur Mitchell's original commitment to the black community by providing social and educational programs."

The *Washington Sunday Times* interviewed a task force member, Brenda Carter, who noted that "one member of our task force is involved with a congregation of almost a thousand people. Community leaders and educators will receive promotional flyers advertising the upcoming engagement, and we'll try to put together some group sales. My husband is in contact with six or seven school principals in the district and he mailed about fifty flyers each to them. They are then stuffing teacher's boxes. A government employee on the task force is distributing the flyers through paycheck envelopes. We also placed flyers on the counters of select stores." Highlighting these grassroots efforts in the media also reinforced the efforts of task force members. Our publicist was very good at bringing the spotlight to these initiatives to expand press coverage and emphasize the validity of partnering with our communities.

New Frontiers in New York City

The national attention garnered by our efforts was gratifying. However, my next big challenge came where I least expected it—New York. In 1992, DTH was scheduled to have its first engagement at Brooklyn Academy of Music (BAM). Buoyed by our recent success outside New York, I continued to look for ways to attract African American audiences to our performances. To my surprise, a plan was created during a routine visit to my doctor—a plan that ultimately resulted in an article by noted dance critic Jennifer Dunning published in the *New York Times* the day we opened ("Harlem Dance Troupe Knocks on Doors to Enlarge Audiences," April 28, 1992). Dunning chronicled our campaign, through which all of BAM's more than 1,900 seats had been sold as a fund-raiser for a scholarship fund sponsored by the Provident Clinical Society (PCS), a then ninety-two-year-old, Brooklyn-based professional organization for black physicians and dentists. Ms. Dunning referred to the fund-raiser as an "innovative marketing" technique for arts organizations.

Indeed, the fund-raiser was a wonderful and challenging experience. As I mentioned, it all started when I went for a checkup with my physician, Dr. Mildred Clark. During my exam, Dr. Clark mentioned that she was the chairperson of PCS's annual fund-raising campaign, which provided scholarships for high school and college students pursuing medical careers. She was looking for a unique fund-raising event. I suggested DTH's opening night at BAM, stressing the fact that PCS would be the first African American organization to buy an opening night of one of our performances. This would be a wonderful way to welcome us to Brooklyn.

Since the opening of the season was still nine months away, we had not yet sold any tickets. I knew this would be a great opportunity for both PCS and DTH to expand in a new direction. Dr. Clark asked me to make a formal presentation to her organization's board, which I did the following month. Using the *60 Minutes* video and persuasive marketing materials, I was able to convince the board that our partnership would be mutually beneficial. But I immediately learned that the organization had never produced an event this large, and that they would need my assistance.

Dr. Clark hired a special events planner, Bessie Edwards, to handle the details for her organization. Over the next six months, I met with Dr. Clark and Ms. Edwards every Tuesday morning at seven A.M. We planned every aspect of the campaign—from awarding scholarships to five local women's health centers, to hosting VIP receptions before and after the performance. The restaurant we chose for the receptions, Two Steps Down, an African American–owned restaurant in the Fort Greene section of Brooklyn (home to numerous artists), was within walking distance of the theatre and could accommodate DTH's traveling photo exhibition. As part of the promotion for the opening season at BAM, the restaurant also made it possible for its diners to fax their ticket requests directly from Two Steps Down to the theatre. (Keep in mind, this was 1992 and fax machines were still relatively new—a real luxury. DTH had just gotten its first fax machine, and we were excited to learn we could use this "advanced technology" to sell tickets!)

Two months before opening night, only 20% of the benefit performance tickets had been sold. Dr. Clark believed the money was not coming in fast enough. She asked all PCS members to solicit contributions for the fund-raiser from the pharmaceutical companies with which they did business. That final push made the difference and, on opening night, the DTH performance at BAM was a sold-out gala! Not only did PCS cover their expenses, the organization had money left over, which is not the case with most fund-raisers. More importantly, at least for DTH, this campaign created a bridge to more than 1,900 African Americans, many who had never before seen a DTH performance.

During DTH's engagement at BAM I learned valuable new lessons in audience cultivation from Virginia Stephens of Allen AME Church in Queens, a mixed-income African American church of about 5,000 members. Through the work at her church, Mrs. Stephens had learned to master the art of ticket-selling. For DTH, in addition to placing an ad for the fund-raiser in her church bulletin, distributing posters and mailing flyers, she also used her personal contacts to sell tickets. She recommended setting up a table in the back of the church so that people could place their ticket orders after services, rather than have to make a special trip to the box office. She even asked for one of the dancer's shoes to use as a prop so that people could get a real sense of what it might be like to stand, walk and dance in a pointe shoe. A simple idea, yet sharing this personal item with the congregation helped demystify dance, creating access for these potential audience members.

While working at the ticket table, I had the opportunity to talk personally with several members of the church and directly address their concerns about the barriers that had kept them from attending cultural events outside their community. One woman thought the protocol for attending a ballet required formal dress, including a fur coat and diamonds. If she didn't dress like that she believed everyone would know she "didn't belong." I assured her that whatever she wore to church would be fine to wear to the ballet. She purchased a ticket.

Mrs. Stephens established a lot of innovative systems to increase ticket sales. She created a method to collect ticket payments in installments, which was the first time this had been done for a DTH performance. She often stated that "people don't like to buy early." Although it took a lot of extra effort to keep track of the payments, Mrs. Stephens was determined that as many people as possible attend a DTH performance at BAM. She encouraged her church committee to constantly distribute personalized flyers; the distributor's name and number were included on the back, so now a potential ticket buyer had a friend that he or she could contact. She established a contact person at other churches, and had these new friends post flyers in highly trafficked areas within their churches. Most churches have fund-raisers throughout the year, and she suggested that the DTH engagement could be presented to the constituents as a way to raise money through ticket sales. Not only did she believe that it was important for her own congregation to support DTH because it was an African American company, she also wanted them to experience the beauty of the art of ballet. She also showed the *60 Minutes* video before lunch at the Allen AME Senior Citizen Center, encouraging the residents to purchase tickets.

Mrs. Stephens did not stop with ticket sales. Concerned about how difficult it was for some of her church members to travel from Queens to Brooklyn, she decided to create a "safe passage" for them. She reserved two cars of the Long Island Railroad so that her people could get on the train near their church in Queens and get off at the train station located half a block from BAM, rather than drive their cars, take the subway or ride the bus. Mrs. Stephens decorated the two LIRR passenger cars with DTH posters and balloons, which we provided. As soon as her members exited the train station, there was another path of balloons leading them to the front door of BAM. What a welcome for her 600 guests!

Together Quilting a New Network

Innovative audience development work requires us to listen and be creative and spontaneous, to always be alert to new opportunities that open doors, create new linkages, build bridges or extend invitations. In February 1992, my friend Peggy Hartwell told me that her monthly quilting group was bored and desperate for a new project. It just so happened that DTH was about to perform for the first time at the New York State Theater at Lincoln Center. I suggested to Peggy that her group (later named and incorporated as Women of Color Quilters Network) use DTH's premiere of six new works as the basis for their next project. I told her that I could provide slides of the new ballets, which could be replicated on their quilts.

After reviewing the slides, the quilting group decided to incorporate all six ballets in one giant work, a quilt that ultimately measured 18 x 24 feet. They worked for free and only asked to be reimbursed for expenses. The group used chiffon, silk, sequins and beads for the dancers' costumes and the dancers' faces were painted by hand, intricately detailed. It took the Women of Color Quilters Network six months to finish the quilt, but as Peggy said: "It is a labor of love."

While the women were working on the quilt, DTH's publicist pitched a story about the quilting project to New York's *Newsday*. The reporter was intrigued by the project, and she wrote a number of feature articles about the quilt. Both groups benefited: the quilting group received press coverage, and a new audience was introduced to DTH. In addition, we were able to tap a brand-new market—the community of craft artisans, many of whom were being exposed to DTH for the first time.

We held a separate reception for the unveiling of the quilt the day before the opening of our performance at Lincoln Center, and extended additional invitations to members of the quilting and crafts communities in the New York area. With the group's permission, we had decided to auction the quilt to raise money for DTH's ballet school. In a silent auction, the quilt sold for $10,000. From the reception's proceeds, we reimbursed the group the $1,000 it spent for supplies. In addition, we gave them tickets to the opening night performance at Lincoln Center, where their work was on display next to the gift shop for the entire two-week run.

Lessons on the International Front

In 1990, DTH performed at the National Cultural Center in Cairo, Egypt—its first appearance on the African continent. I went to Cairo in advance of the rest of the company to work with the presenter on a marketing campaign. We wanted to ensure that as many people as possible had access to tickets. The Cultural Center has 1,000 seats, the majority of which are sold to upper-class and elite ticket buyers. The remaining 15 million Caireens rarely go to the theatre because of the prohibitive price. In a meeting with local artists, the presenter and I decided to create a number of outreach events so that more people could see DTH perform. Working with the U.S. embassy in Cairo, we were able to arrange a broadcast of the *60 Minutes* segment on a local network. An estimated 10 million people saw the program. The presenter assisted us in hosting several panel discussions on a variety of topics in different communities, such as drug abuse and the need for artists to take care of their bodies. We also visited local dance schools to encourage young students to develop and pursue their dreams.

In Cairo, I learned that there are many aspects to and options for exposing the public to the arts. It does not always have to be a performance. Here was a situation where we could not change the economic reality of who would have access to theatre, but we could certainly work around it to accomplish our goal of embracing all people, despite class and economic differences. Location, access and resources are all factors that need to be considered. More important, rather than wait for anyone else to create the right programs and opportunities, I realized that it was up to me to discover the right point of entry for each audience member and then create it.

The Healing Power of Art in South Africa

It took two years of negotiations, but on September 1, 1992, DTH arrived in Johannesburg, South Africa. The company had been invited to perform at the reopening of the newly renovated Civic Theatre, an internationally recognized venue for touring productions from around the world. The country was in the early stages of dismantling its decades-old apartheid policies on the heels of Nelson Mandela's release from prison, and DTH was to be the first American company to perform in South Africa after a 30-year cultural ban had been lifted. Mr. Mitchell had been very strict about the terms of the contract. He insisted that there be an integrated technical crew and that the audience be integrated with black South Africans, which would be a first for the Civic Theatre. He also insisted that the presenters help sponsor outreach activities to black South African schools in the townships.

Three months before the opening, I was dispatched to Johannesburg to work with the presenters to set up the publicity campaign. Had I really thought about the political climate and what kind of resistance I might encounter because I'm African American, I might have declined. Instead, I saw it as another opportunity to do audience development work, another opportunity to learn something new. In preparation for my trip, I gathered several gifts from DTH—jackets, sweatshirts and caps. I learned long ago that giving gifts (when the act is sincere) is a great way to break the ice.

My first meeting at the theatre to plan the campaign for the DTH tour was with twenty-two white South Africans who were involved in various aspects of marketing the tour. When I walked into the room, I immediately sensed tremendous hostility and discomfort. Even though I believed their feelings stemmed from their misguided views about blacks (whom generations of white South Africans had been taught were inferior), I refused to let it get in the way of the important work I knew I was there to do. I realized that their country was changing quickly, and that the culture of apartheid was being challenged not only by the release of Mr. Mandela, but also by the performance of DTH and the terms of our contract requiring integrated audiences. However, I truly believed then, as I still do, that the healing powers of the arts are unparalleled. I had a purpose—to develop the best, most effective and inclusive marketing campaign, one that would embrace black South Africans in a manner they had never experienced before. As I prepared for my presentation and continued to study the people in the room, I momentarily thought that maybe I had been overzealous about the potential impact DTH could have in South Africa. Perhaps I had totally overlooked the possibility that the country might not yet be ready for what we were proposing. But in my gut, I knew that it was time for the situation to change, and my being there meant that I had an important role to play in that process.

When everybody was quiet and settled, I took a deep breath and smiled. I was determined that we establish a level of mutual respect, that we work together to ensure that the DTH tour was a success. As I passed out the DTH gifts, the people in the room began to relax, and it was easier to move forward. By the end of my week of preparation, the presenters were enthusiastically engaged in the marketing campaign and had hired a black South African advertising agency to design the posters and flyers. Even the white South African secretaries who initially ignored me were asking to fax or type up my notes and serving me tea.

You never know where your work will take you. I certainly never anticipated that my efforts to develop audiences would take me to South Africa—a nation struggling with its racial policies—to help integrate a theatre. But I learned that when you are prepared and understand all of the aspects of strategically planned audience development, you can transplant those skills and tools and make them work anywhere in the world. So what I did around the country and in New York, I began to do in Johannesburg.

Later on, we would discover one major obstacle in accomplishing our goal of integrating the audiences for the evening performances. Black South Africans were required by law to be in their homes by ten every night. That meant they could come to matinees but not to evening performances. The performance times had already been set and could not be changed to allow for an earlier curtain, and we could not alter the law in the short period of time remaining. So rather than excluding black South Africans from our show, we created more than 250 outreach activities and took our show directly into the townships.

Even this well-intentioned effort, however, sparked some controversy. As an article in *Newsday* (September 1, 1992) noted: "The tour, which is costing $1.1 million of predominantly private money, has raised the ire of some South African dancers who believe that the funds would have been better spent invested in existing companies and projects in the country . . . You could save about 90% of the money . . . and create jobs within, said a high-ranking official of the Performing Arts Council. The Dance Theatre's backers dispute such claims. They cite Mitchell's extensive community outreach programs as one of the primary reasons the troupe was invited in the first place."

I was met with the impact of long-felt hostility toward the South African government and resentment over decades of institutionalized racism when I met with local dance companies in hopes of crafting beneficial partnerships. I set out to make sure the local dance companies knew we saw our presence as a cultural *exchange* that would include extensive community outreach programs. We not only wanted to share our resources and knowledge of the classics; we also wanted to learn from them. As a result of this dialogue, we were able to develop partnerships with local artists and arts groups. The dance companies served as our bridge by helping us plan and implement our outreach activities. By listening to their concerns, creating outreach events that displayed their dance style and ours, and offering master classes and seminars in their communities, we were able to develop mutual respect for each other's mission (an example of using soft power). This relationship became a true cultural exchange. Many members of our company were able to learn the South African boot dance, which was added to DTH's repertoire, in addition to an original piece called *South African Suite*. We learned about South African culture and established a scholarship fund and a student exchange program. We were able to hire our education director through this program.

With the assistance of these local dance companies, DTH was able to perform in five black townships around the country as well as to hold 250 master classes and workshops over a three-week period. DTH members taught classes in vacant lots, in front yards or in community centers. (Whenever we met children, we danced for them!) All of our staff got involved—our tech crew held workshops on sound and lighting, our musicians held workshops on musical scoring, and members of our board of directors, who had accompanied the dancers on tour, held workshops on development issues. I presented a workshop on developing marketing strategies for the staff at the Market Theatre in Johannesburg, because apartheid had limited black South African access to current information and resources.

The full impact of my efforts in South Africa hit me at the very end of my trip, when the sponsor gave me a tour of the Civic Theatre, where the stage was being readied for DTH's arrival. As I entered the stage, the black workmen, one by one, put down their tools, stood up and stared at me. "Do you know what they are doing?" my white escort asked.

"No," I replied, trying not to feel self-conscious as the ten men stared at me without speaking or smiling.

"They are paying homage to you," my escort explained. "They are honoring you. You are the first black person to enter this theatre who is free, not a worker, but an individual."

New York's ABC News sent reporter Roz Abrams to accompany the dancers on their South Africa tour. She documented the entire trip, from DTH's arrival at the theatre to the performances in the townships. When the dancers returned home, many of them said the trip to South Africa had been the most rewarding, fulfilling and exhausting tour they had ever performed. We were able to successfully accomplish our goal of breaking down some of the barriers of apartheid through the arts.

When Nelson Mandela, then president of the African National Congress, attended the opening performance, he met with the dancers at a reception. They were deeply touched by his comments:

> It is occasions like this that make us forget about the hard knocks which we continue to receive in life . . . We have forgotten about all those problems tonight because Dance

Nelson Mandela (left) with Dance Theatre of Harlem.

Theatre of Harlem has taught us lessons which are more significant than a group of artists coming to our country and performing . . . As I look at them, I am reminded of the words of a poet who said: "In the rough marble, beauty hides unseen—in the still air, music lays unheard." There is nothing rough about them; there is only beauty. At least for a few hours tonight, we were able to forget all these things, and we were transported on a wave of happiness, which has put us in peace with the entire world.

The generosity of the many dancers, arts administrators and presenters helped to lay a foundation for change. These marvelous innovations were the result of collaborative ideas and efforts, and also of establishing an arena for creativity in which the entire community could flourish.

Chapter 5

CULTURAL EXPLOSIONS: THE PUBLIC THEATER

If there is no struggle, there is no progress.
—FREDERICK DOUGLASS

It started with a message on my answering machine: "This is George Wolfe," the voice said.

I had never met George C. Wolfe, but I knew his work. He had recently become Producer of The Public Theater/New York Shakespeare Festival, one of the nation's leading theatre institutions. The Public, one of the country's leading not-for-profit theatres, had a long list of Broadway credits, including *Hair* and *A Chorus Line*; under founder Joseph Papp it was also one of the first theatres in the country to stage Shakespeare with nontraditional casting. The "supporting cast" of actors who worked at The Public over the years included Academy, Obie and Tony award–winning actors, such as Meryl Streep, Denzel Washington, Al Pacino, Savion Glover, Angela Bassett, Kevin

Kline, Christopher Walken, Colleen Dewhurst, Gloria Foster and Raul Julia. The arrival of writer and director George Wolfe to serve as the organization's producer heralded even more excitement for the future. It had been impossible for me to get tickets to his first play, which was produced at The Public, the critically acclaimed *The Colored Museum*, due to its box-office success. But I had seen the Broadway production of *Jelly's Last Jam*, which he wrote (with lyricist Susan Birkenhead) and directed, four times. After the last performance, I told myself that one day I would meet George C. Wolfe.

"I want to talk to you," the message continued. "Please give me a call."

The following week we met in his office at The Public. I felt honored that Mr. Wolfe wanted to discuss audience development issues with me. "I want to create an American theatre that looks and feels like the people we serve," he said during our meeting. "Our audience should look like a subway stop in New York City. To do that we have to create a program that not only brings people into the theatre, but also *serves* the community." I suggested that he might want to launch an audience development initiative that would involve the theatre proactively, reaching out to every segment of the community not currently involved with The Public. He smiled, nodded, and said he would think about it. Our meeting ended.

On the subway ride home, I began to think about what a great opportunity it would be for me to work at The Public and with George C. Wolfe, even though there had been no discussion about a position. Over the next week, I researched the theatre and its activities. The more information I found, the more I knew that this was the job for me, in a place where I believed I could really make a difference. I sent Mr. Wolfe a two-page proposal about what I would do if he hired me to head his audience development initiative. My proposal included targeting the Asian, African American and Latino communities in order to create partnerships with the theatre, and I made suggestions for cultivating younger audiences.

A couple of weeks passed before I heard from Mr. Wolfe again. He asked me to come back to The Public for a meeting. He told me he was forming a new department that did not exist at any other theatre. "I'd like to you be the director of this department. Think of a name," he said. I immediately accepted the challenge and suggested that the department be called "community affairs."

One of the first things I did, even before I reported for my first day of work, was attend a staff meeting. I explained my goals and outlined how I believed they could be accomplished. Next, I made a similar presentation to the theatre's board of directors. After these meetings, both the staff and the board were committed to the effort. I learned from this that if you want to make something happen, it is imperative that you help everyone understand exactly what you're trying to do, what your needs and expectations are, and what the benefits will be for the organization. You have to be both passionate and detailed about your goals so that the staff, board and, eventually, the community will rally behind your efforts. They must believe you can make it happen, and they must want to share in your achievements.

During my first week on the job, George (as everyone called him) issued a press release to announce The Public Theater's new initiative:

> As part of his initiative to expand and diversify theatre audiences, New York Shakespeare Festival producer George C. Wolfe has recently appointed Donna Walker-Kuhne to head the newly created Department of Community Affairs and Group Sales . . . The department will serve to break down barriers of unfamiliarity and misconceptions among communities who have little or no contact with the theatre world. The program will offer a range of public relations and outreach activities that extend into the five boroughs.
>
> Ms. Walker-Kuhne will open the program with "Cultural Explosions," an aggressive and proactive group sales campaign geared toward attracting specific minority groups . . . "Cultural Explosions" will introduce theatre audiences to productions that reflect their own cultures and encourage crossover among audiences to the diverse programming available at The Public Theater.

It was official—the word was on the street. I had to get to work! First, I needed a staff. George recommended Irene Cabrera and Barbara Tran, and, after interviewing them, I was glad to welcome them to my team. Although neither had any marketing experience, I was impressed by their strong sense of ethnic pride, enthusiasm, intelligence and creativity. Also, Lakota Collier, my former intern from DTH, called me to ask if she could join my department. I was delighted. Despite my extensive background in audience development with DTH, working in the theatre was an entirely new experience, and I felt as if I were taking a crash course. This was not a situation in which the plans were already mapped out for us. We were starting from zero and had a very short time to get

up to speed. The first four months would prove to be crucial. The strong philosophical base and artistic vision George had outlined for us—a vision that was woven into the fabric of the institution—contributed to our effectiveness. He made it very clear to the staff, the board and the community leaders with whom he would come in contact that diversifying The Public Theater's audiences was his primary objective.

I believe George was seeking to restore The Public's reputation as a "people's theatre," in keeping with the legacy of its founder, Joseph Papp. After founding The Public, Papp explained (in *Joe Papp: An American Life* by Helen Epstein, Little, Brown and Company, New York, 1994), "I wanted to reach audiences who might never have seen a play before . . . audiences who were unable or unwilling to pay." The Emmanuel Church on East Sixth Street in Manhattan was the first venue for his early theatrical performances. But he soon noticed that the audience did not seem comfortable. "Was it because they were in a church and felt compelled to dress up?" he wondered. "Or was it because they were sitting amongst strangers?"

To test this theory, he moved his productions to the East River Amphitheater. There the shows attracted Puerto Ricans, Italians, African Americans, Chinese people and Jews, newly arrived immigrants who lived on the Lower East Side. During a performance of *Julius Caesar*, the crowd cheered. Mr. Papp was bowled over by the response and was delighted that the audience really identified with the work.

By the end of the first summer of outdoor productions, a pair of Shakespeare plays had been performed before more than 2,500 people. Mr. Papp had an agreement with the Parks Department that if his plays at the East River Amphitheater were a success, the productions could travel to other boroughs. The following summer, his Festival Mobile Theater became a source of fascination for audiences and critics alike. *New Yorker* magazine writer J. M. Flagler captured the diversity of the audiences when he wrote of one performance: "In front of me sat three generations of an Italian family, in back of me were two old ladies chattering in part-Yiddish, part-English, part-Italian."

Another Papp innovation was nontraditional, multiracial casting. In 1955, blacks were scarce on Broadway and scarcer still in classical performances. Mainstream theatre meant "white" theatre performed by white actors. But anybody could walk into Mr. Papp's actor workshops and feel welcome. Actors, critics and the public soon became intrigued by Mr. Papp's vision of "an American kind of Shakespeare." The multiracial casting that has been a hallmark of The Public's productions over the past half-century continues to reflect Papp's passion for a genuine and diverse American theatre.

A documentary about Joe Papp's life contains footage of him talking through a bullhorn as he walks through neighborhoods to promote his Shakespeare in the Park productions. His invitation was personal, warm and sincere. The documentary also shows his diverse working-class audience. It was as a result of that documentary that I recognized my department's responsibility for continuing the legacy that Mr. Papp created almost fifty years before.

The First Ninety Days

My staff and I spent the first ninety days in our new department of community affairs and group sales conducting research. We consulted community leaders and contacted people through organization directories, religious directories and telephone directories. We asked: "Why haven't you been to The Public? Is it the price of the tickets? The productions? The theatre's perspective?" The answers to those questions directed our next steps. Usually we followed up by scheduling meetings: one of the keys to successful audience development is face-to-face, life-to-life and heart-to-heart contact. During the initial phases of our outreach campaign, my staff and I were only in the office long enough to set up appointments and maintain written correspondence. The rest of the time, we were working in the field.

I want to make an important point: The Public did not launch its department of community affairs to create small groups of ethnic-specific audiences or youth-specific audiences. That is both boring and backward-thinking. Our interest was to create an opportunity for all of the city's cultures and groups to intersect, connect and, in

George's vision, *collide*. In order for this to happen, we had to first make sure people were comfortable with our institution and our product. Often that meant making something available at the theatre with which they were already familiar, such as activities sponsored by organizations from their own communities. That led to opportunities to provide them with newer experiences.

Initially, some people were suspicious. Several cultural organizations told us they had been contacted by other "white arts institutions" under the pretense of working together, and that after sharing their mailing lists with those institutions, they never heard from them again. At one meeting, after our introduction, the executive director stood up and announced that she would not participate in "cultural appropriation." She walked out of the room. I was stunned by her reaction—especially since I believed that The Public was trying to build bridges and open its doors, not "appropriate" anything. However, I realized that we were stepping into a quagmire of disillusion and mistrust based on her perceptions of how her organization had been treated previously by other institutions. We had two choices: either give up or develop the patience it would take to create new relationships. Given our mandate, we knew what had to be done. My staff and I later talked about the importance of having a strong sense of purpose, a strong will and an invincible spirit, so that we could openly listen to the concerns being expressed by these skeptical organizations. We talked about the power of the arts to transcend differences and the bigger picture of a mutual partnership. That bumpy beginning actually turned out to be a great benefit. It forced us to develop a presentation that was more inviting, which allowed more time for listening and engaging in dialogue.

It definitely takes a certain personality to do audience development work. If you are the type of person who is easily offended, you should select someone else to handle it. The goal of these interactions is to develop institutional awareness—to help your prospective partners and audiences get to know who you are and what your institution stands for. The only way you can do that is by becoming open, visible and accessible.

We began our subsequent meetings by passing out gifts—T-shirts, mugs and posters—as a token of our appreciation for those who took the time to meet with us. As I had learned working with DTH, this usually proves a successful first point of entry. We also shared George's vision about the kind of theatre we hoped The Public could become: a place filled with audiences that reflected the city of New York, and a theatre where programs and productions embraced and resonated with the stories of the city's diverse people. Our goal in initiating these dialogues was not to acquire anything from them, but to establish mutual trust. We wanted to build a foundation in each of these communities so that everyone could come to see The Public as their own theatre.

After we met with several organizations, a number of wonderful things began to happen. They began to *offer* to share their resources, such as their mailing lists, because they saw and felt the sincerity of our efforts. This happened because we patiently built the foundation, without the expectation that we would receive anything in return.

Making Everyone Welcome

With the launch of our new audience development initiative, George also believed it was important that The Public revamp its image. He hired a new design team, led by the cutting-edge designer Paula Scher, to graphically capture the new spirit of The Public. Her agency, Pentagram, created a new logo, which became a part of all our materials, from the signage in the lobby to our programs and brochures. New red leather furniture and brighter lights were added to the lobby, making it an even more inviting place to enter, sit and relax.

In addition, George became involved with the house staff. As part of our audience development initiative, he wanted to make sure that from the moment our guests walked in the front door, someone who was happy to be working at The Public greeted them. George hired bilingual, Spanish-speaking house staff to lessen the challenge of language barriers. More importantly, he made sure that the entire house staff—from ushers and box-office people to the technical crew and the janitors—was fully aware of every aspect of the audience development initiative, and he solicited their input. Their suggestions proved invaluable. Because the initiative was a theatre-wide objective, my department was able to establish flexible purchasing procedures and ticket payment options with the box-office staff. These new ticket procedures eventually enabled us to achieve a 10% increase in box-office receipts.

You may not always be in a position to guarantee that the programming is going to be totally satisfying or enjoyable to a particular set of patrons, but you can brand the institution and develop audience loyalty by creating an ambiance that supersedes whatever they see onstage or posted on the walls. You can do that by making sure that your guests are treated well, no matter what. Ultimately you want the community you serve to see your institution as a cultural watering hole, the place they can go any time they need or want to have their thirst for performance and art satisfied. You want them to be able to say: "This is my place. I know the staff, they make me feel welcome." It makes me happy to see our guests sitting in the lobby reading, having lunch or chatting with friends. They are not there for a play or panel discussion, they are just hanging out because they feel welcome.

Opening Up the House

Three months after my staff and I began our "Cultural Explosions" campaign, we held an "Open House" celebration (which has since become an annual event). We invited all the people we had been talking to about The Public, during our research phase, to an open-door event involving The Public's entire complex. Invitations were sent to approximately 700 people.

The theme of our "Open House" was exploring, respecting and appreciating cultures from around the world, and we turned our landmark building into a world stage. The lobby was decorated in bright colors with bold graphics and bright lights. There were Native American, Cuban, African and Korean drummers playing in the lobby as our guests arrived. There was a food table representing every cuisine imaginable.

Our guests included religious leaders, group leaders, educators, and the heads of social and professional groups. The "Open House" served as a major point of entry for many of our new friends, who were introduced to The Public and its history through guided tours of all its five theatres and the lobby area. There were approximately seven simultaneous group tours led by staff members. Our guests were very excited when one of the tour guides announced: "You are now standing on the stage where *Hair* was first performed." There were more "ohhhs" and "ahhhs" when our guests found themselves in the theatre where *A Chorus Line* had been performed. Giving everyone the opportunity to stand on The Public's stage created a bridge between the past and the present, and from the present to the future.

During George's welcoming remarks, he explained his vision for The Public and talked about the upcoming season. He likened The Public's productions to a restaurant menu. "You're walking down the street and you pass your favorite restaurant," he said. "As you pass by, the aroma of your favorite dish is so strong that you have to go inside and order it. You're too hungry to take it home. So you sit down and eat it and it tastes good! Since you're there, you decide, 'Maybe I'll try another dish.' The first dish was so satisfying, you're confident that other dishes on the menu will be, too. That's how we want you to think about The Public. We want to be your favorite *cultural* restaurant. Come and feast, and we will feast with you."

Before our guests left, we asked them to fill out a survey. If they did, they were given a gift bag. The surveys told us a lot about what people thought of our institution and what they wanted to see. Comments included requests for new plays as well as more Shakespeare. Many also mentioned that they were pleased to hear about the "Cultural Explosions" campaign and intended to come back. Several offered to volunteer. We added this information to our research database.

As we followed up with each person who attended the "Open House," we were excited to learn that the community was abuzz about

The Public. Because we had invited them to our house "to play," created a warm and exciting environment, introduced them to our staff, who made them feel welcome and at ease, shared our vision with them and helped them talk and network with each other, The Public suddenly had become the place to go. The "Open House" laid the foundation for the forging of a collaborative energy between The Public and our new community partners. This was the first turning point in our audience development efforts.

The next step we took was to design a vehicle that would help us maintain ongoing communication. We created a newsletter called *Inside the Public.* The eight-page, quarterly publication contained information about the season and featured updates on community affairs activities. Then we followed up with a direct-mail campaign, sending letters to let our community know what was coming up next. These mailings were targeted to specific cultural interests: We focused on the African American, Latino and Asian communities and those productions in which they might be particularly interested.

Sharing Our Space

We created another point of entry by making our space available, for free, to a variety of our community partners for fund-raisers, board meetings and staged readings. Some groups attending performances also held pre- or post-performance receptions, and cast members or the playwright would attend when possible. A black literary organization based in Washington, D.C., even held its annual board meeting at The Public, though only one of its members actually lived in New York.

We formally welcomed each group, using the opportunity to talk about our ongoing events at The Public. We encouraged all of our visitors to sign our mailing list. It became a mutual exchange of information and a sharing of resources. It was part of our effort to make The Public more accessible and available to the community.

Being Prepared to Take Action

Once you open your door to input, you must be prepared to take action. It is important not to be insensitive or to ignore what people say about your institution (good or bad). This was one of the many lessons I learned in 1993, when I took George uptown to meet with some artistic leaders in Harlem. I chose Harlem for several reasons. First and foremost, because it was rare at that time for a major arts institution to go to Harlem to have a dialogue with its artistic community. Second, I was very familiar with all the organizations and leaders and felt quite certain we could have an open and honest exchange. My goal was to build a cultural bridge from Harlem to The Public. We sat in a circle and began to talk.

"How can The Public support you?" George asked.

"We would like some Shakespeare up here," one man responded. "Nobody ever does Shakespeare in Harlem!" Everyone in the room nodded their heads.

"We'll look into that," he said. "Is there anything else?" For an intense half hour, Harlem's cultural leaders shared their concerns and stories of their struggles to build and maintain audiences, as well as attract financial support. George listened intently. I took notes. As the meeting wrapped up, George made a closing point: "There's something I would like to see you do," George said. "I think all the arts organizations in Harlem should meet on a regular basis to program work so that productions don't happen simultaneously. Currently, your audiences don't know what to see because there are ten plays all on the first Friday and then nothing else the rest of the month."

A new program, "Shakespeare in Harlem," was launched by The Public in August 1994 as a direct response to our meeting. First, we established a free workshop in which Harlem-based actors could work with other African American actors on the physical and language demands of Shakespearean performance. We learned that the thought of performing Shakespeare intimidated many of them—they thought they needed to be able to imitate a British accent or that performing

Shakespeare required some type of personality adaptation. The Public's workshop helped modify those preconceptions. Very quickly the Harlem-based actors were performing scenes as if by second nature. I'm not suggesting they immediately mastered the text, but they did break through the barrier that had been blocking them from even attempting the work until that point.

George also scheduled a workshop for Harlem-based directors. This was held at the Schomburg Center for Research in Black Culture. It was a magical afternoon in which George (a masterful director himself) shared secrets of the trade with experienced and novice directors.

Then we planned a free public performance of a series of Shakespearean monologues. Curated by George, the performance, held at the Victoria V Theatre on West 125th Street, featured African American actors Regina Taylor, Keith David, LisaGay Hamilton and Tamara Tunie. My staff and I handled the media outreach and marketing of the event. We were astonished by the public response. More than 400 people attended, primarily young adults and children. The reading, which lasted well over an hour, was followed by an equally long Q&A session. When the program ended the audience gave everyone a five-minute standing ovation—no one wanted to leave.

We also worked with the Harlem arts leaders to form an ad hoc group called "Extending Today's Audience." The late Joseph Persons, who was head of the Harlem Cultural Council at the time, and I invited various artists and theatre leaders to meet on a monthly basis to talk about programming and marketing. In 1997, the group held its first annual summer arts festival, featuring various performances from different Harlem-based organizations. The Public provided marketing assistance and featured our Shakespeare in Harlem program. Today this organization, under the new name "Harlem Arts Alliance," continues its monthly meetings and activities and provides technical, marketing and administrative support. Under the creative direction of producer Voza Rivers, it also serves as a point of entry into the art and cultural landscape of Harlem.

These programs grew out of our initial dialogue with Harlem's cultural leaders. We listened to their requests, created programs that facilitated our mutual goals and built a bridge between The Public and Harlem. We discovered that Shakespeare is a valuable tool for diversifying audiences. "Shakespeare in Harlem" is now an annual event, and similar programs (geared toward teens and young adults) have been established in Brooklyn, the Bronx and Queens.

A Showcase for Our Partners

Many cultural groups with whom we spoke wanted to have a presence at The Public. My staff and I knew we were entering dangerous territory by discussing programming, but we promised to share their concerns with The Public's literary department. Out of this discussion grew a new monthly program: "Free at Three," which gave our new cultural partners a forum to showcase their own work to their constituents. The arrangement was simple: The Public provided the space, marketing support, mailings (based on the participating partner's lists) and staff. To enhance our effectiveness, the cultural partner was the co-host for each event. Each invitation, program and news release came from The Public and our cultural partner. This gave them a sense of ownership for the program, sending a message that we were *partners* in the venture. The cultural partners provided the product— poetry, music, dance, staged readings, even a health and healing event—with The Public Theater staff in a curatorial role. (Although the health and healing program didn't have to do with theatre directly, we felt it was important to step outside what felt "safe" in order to embrace the ideas the community was sharing with us.) Each event ended with the promotion of our next program, so we were always promoting forward. We offered discounted tickets for future productions. Our goal was to get people into the building—the first step toward cultivating relationships and developing programming specific to their needs.

"Free at Three" provided us with opportunities to set up programs related to *our* productions, while providing a forum for our new audiences through dialogue and interchange. We used a panel format developed with our cultural partners, featuring playwrights, actors and/or critics. Over the course of eight years, we held more than 100 "Free at Three" programs, working with a wonderful group of cultural collaborators to create events such as:

- "Bamboo Girls, Bhangra Music and Yellow Pride"—a panel discussion of first- and second-generation Asian American youth exploring their identity and culture through zines, music and other alternative media, organized around The Public's production of Philip Kan Gotanda's *Ballad of Yachiyo*, and held in collaboration with the Museum of Chinese in the Americas.
- "Seizing the Time: A New Generation of Protest Poetry," hosted by the famed founder of Nuyorican Poets Cafe, Miguel Algarin. The performances of NPC illustrated injustice, racial inequality and the need for cultural expression. This "Free at Three" program was presented in conjunction with our 1997 production of Roger Guenveur Smith's one-man play *A Huey P. Newton Story*, about the life of one of the founding members of the Black Panther Party. It featured hip-hop and R&B music by emerging artists, a great fit for the 18- to 30-year-old audience that brought such an energetic atmosphere to the performances.
- "Democracy in the 21st Century" was organized in conjunction with Anna Deavere Smith's play *House Arrest*, which explores the role of the presidency in American history and the impact of the press on politics in the White House. The discussion, scheduled after one of Ms. Smith's matinee performances in the 2000 season, featured an illustrious panel of journalists and academicians. However, Ms. Smith's voice was suffering from strain after the two-and-a-half hour, one-woman show, and she was instructed by her doctor not to speak. The discussion had been set up months in advance and the house was packed. Ms. Smith and I felt she needed to make an appearance, even if she did not speak, so she decided to write down all of her comments on notepads. The audi-

ence was delighted. Remember: The show must go on! It's always important not to miss an opportunity to spread your message, especially when the room is full of people who are ready to listen. Be creative and see it through.

One especially important and unique alliance we formed was with the publication *Callaloo*, a scholarly journal on African American literature. George met Editor Charles Rowell while on vacation in Brazil. They struck up a conversation, and George suggested that Charles contact me when he returned to the States. When Charles called, we were in the process of planning our fall season and monthly "Free at Three" schedules. We decided to have *Callaloo* co-sponsor our season-opening event, which was a free reading by gay African American playwrights. *Callaloo* provided us with its mailing list. The crowd was incredibly diverse, and the event was so popular that we had to turn people away. The *Callaloo* staff sold copies of the journal at the event and we distributed information about our upcoming season. The event was so successful that we went on to co-host a "Free at Three" program with *Callaloo* every year.

One program that didn't work was "Whose History? A Hip-Hop Perspective," organized in collaboration with New York University's African Studies program. We described the panel this way: "A new generation of black artists are excavating history and giving the cultural artifacts they find a fresh, irreverent spin." It was tied to our 1996 production of Robert O'Hara's *Insurrection: Holding History*, an ambitious play about a 189-year-old former slave who takes his great-great-grandson back in time to Nat Turner's ill-fated rebellion. Based on our description, the audience attending this "Free at Three" event assumed the discussion would be about hip-hop music and expected to hear some live music. Hip-hop's popularity was greatly increasing, and reaching out to the student population with this language suggested that P. Diddy and crew would all be there. Despite the prestigious panel, which included writer James Hannaham and artist Kara Walker, the audience began leaving in large numbers before the program was even half over. I realized that we had not been clear in describing the event in our marketing materials, and consequently the audience was disappointed. Remember: It's always important to be specific, never ambiguous, in your marketing materials. You want the right people at your event, and getting them through the doors at the wrong time could be worse than never opening the doors at all.

In 2000, George encouraged my department to expand the original concept of "Free at Three" in order to further explore the issues and cultural backgrounds of the diverse communities the theatre serves. These monthly programs became known as "Conversations with . . ." and always highlighted salient issues from current productions. They were designed to serve as a direct bridge from the audience to the production.

This new mandate also required that my department expand our roster of possible participants. How did we find new candidates? We developed an ongoing relationship with PEN American Center, a literary research organization. We also broadened our research to study trends in art and culture to ascertain who were the cultural tastemakers and what issues were they addressing. In addition, we attended panel discussions hosted by the *New York Times* and other prominent organizations.

Reaching Out to Asian American Audiences

For several consecutive years in the 1990s, The Public had not produced an Asian American play. What could we say to these group leaders with whom we had spent considerable time cultivating relationships and building interest in our theatre? It's true, we could have encouraged them to see other kinds of plays and, in some instances, we did. But we believed that first-time audience members wanted and needed to see how we were reaching out to *them*.

After brainstorming sessions, my staff came up with other ideas to get the Asian American community into the theatre. Many of the ideas involved a policy we had already implemented—making our space available free of charge. We worked with several organizations, including the Asian American Arts Alliance, the Asian American Legal Defense and Education Fund, and Asian American Writers' Workshop, to make it possible for them to hold readings, fund-raisers and special events at The Public. In this way, the partners became the bridge for first-time audiences to come to the theatre to interact with organizations with whom they were already familiar.

My associate, Janice Pono, also invited several Asian arts organizations to host their events at The Public throughout the year. These primarily Filipino arts groups—writers, actors, musicians and students—held planning meetings, readings and fund-raisers at the theatre on a regular basis. This enhanced the visibility of smaller organizations with their boards of directors and their constituents, as well as with potential funding sources. The space was provided pro bono; staff costs were usually under $200, which made it affordable. Having these events at The Public gave us the opportunity to maintain an ongoing dialogue with these groups in an effort to build future audiences.

In the winter of 1999, Janice also suggested to our literary department that The Public host a weeklong Asian Writers Conference during our annual New Work Now! Festival, a popular series of staged readings over a two-week period. The Asian Writers Conference presented excerpts from *every* play written by an Asian playwright that had ever been produced by The Public. Sandwiched between the readings were performances by spoken-word artists, panel discussions and music. Prominent Asian American playwrights, including David Henry Hwang (*M. Butterfly*), Alice Tuan (*Ajax, por nobody*), Jessica Hagedorn (*Dogeaters*) and Chay Yew (*A Language of Their Own*), participated in the conference. Numerous actors and heads of Asian theatre companies also attended. There were receptions after each event, during which audience members and panelists continued their dialogue.

We saw this writers conference as an opportunity to acknowledge the worthwhile contributions of Asian artists, especially to the theatre community. The standing-room-only event also showed us that there was tremendous interest in this work.

The success of the writers conference helped influence the theatre's decision to produce Jessica Hagedorn's epic *Dogeaters*, a play based on her novel about her experiences in the Philippines during the 1980s under the Marcos regime. Developed at the Sundance Theatre Lab, the play version of *Dogeaters* had its world premier at La Jolla Playhouse in 1998, and had its New York debut at The Public during the 2000 season. While preparing our audience development campaign for *Dogeaters*, we reached out to many Asian American organizations we had been working with over the past several years. Because Hagedorn (a teacher and multimedia artist as well as a writer) is a beloved figure in the educational and arts communities, especially in New York, several of her former students volunteered to help market her show.

Despite the fact that Janice Pono had moved to Thailand before *Dogeaters* premiered, she had established a solid base for The Public within the Filipino community. Consequently, my remaining staff was able to follow up and expand on her efforts. Preparation for *Dogeaters* began in the summer of 2000 for a scheduled February 2001 opening. My interns spent considerable time outlining events that would help us cultivate audiences, developing topics for panel discussions, finding locations for flyer distribution and identifying sources for advertising, as well as cultivating "tastemakers" who would help spread the word. We also met with the playwright several times to share ideas and get her input.

This collaboration was a formula for success. As a result of our efforts, our community affairs department was able to generate more than 35% of the box-office income during the seven-week run of *Dogeaters*. By coding our discount flyers and by directing group sales through my department, we could measure all ticket sales that resulted from our efforts. (I return to the group sales initiatives for this production later in this chapter.)

Revelations in Music: Opening the Door to Latino Audiences

Even for Latino-themed plays, developing crossover audiences can be difficult. In a *New York Times* article ("The Tricky Business of Cross-Cultural Theatre," Feb. 27, 2001), reporter Mireya Navarro notes the challenges of developing Latino audiences. Referring to the Off-Broadway musical *4 Guys Named José . . . and una Mujer Named María!*, she writes that "finding an audience in New York has not been easy. The experience of *4 Guys* underscores the challenges of creating and marketing theatre, whose traditional audience is largely white, not only to different audiences but to the diversity within those audiences, the Latino one being a prime case in point." The production had to appeal to Spanish- and English-speaking audiences, as well as "diverse Hispanic groups, which often gravitate toward theatre from their own countries." To enhance the crossover appeal of *4 Guys*, Navarro writes that playwright Delores Prida "selected songs by composers from Mexico, Puerto Rico, Cuba and the Dominican Republic, four major nationalities well represented in this country's Latino population."

Although The Public was producing the works of several Latino artists, we were not drawing in Latino audiences in substantial numbers and we were not sure why. So we went back to our "tastemakers" and began to ask questions: "What do you think about this? Is it interesting? What kind of response can we expect? How should we present it?" As a result of this informal survey, we discovered that the subject matter of one of the plays we had presented, *Blade to the Heat*, was offensive to many older Latino audience members because it dealt with a gay lifestyle in the macho Latino boxing community. This subject was not widely discussed within the older age group that seemed most interested in attending plays at The Public (even though Oliver Mayer's play was brilliant and everyone who saw it loved it). Once we received information about our audience's concerns, we switched gears. Rather than putting our energy into pulling in our traditional Latino audience, we went after a younger demographic. The tool we used was music.

We applied this strategy to the next Latino play we produced, *Dancing on Her Knees* by Nilo Cruz (who went on to receive the Pulitzer Prize for Drama in 2003 for *Anna in the Tropics*). The producer of the music group Dark Latin Groove called to inquire about the possibility of his group performing at one of our music events. After several meetings, we decided to curate a panel discussion exploring different types of Latino music, with Dark Latin Groove and other bands performing live. We planned a reception, serving chicken, rice, beans and plantains. The line of predominantly young Latinos that wrapped around the block that day was proof of our success—we had to rent video monitors to accommodate the overflow in our lobby. It was clear that music was a key component in facilitating our invitation to the Latino community.

Because of this success, we solicited the assistance of the late (and at the time very popular) promoter and producer Ana Araiz. We began programming a series of Latino music panels featuring live music as part of our "Free at Three" series. One of the most popular events (300 people were in attendance) showcased Cuban music of the 1950s. It was hosted by actor Kamar de los Reyes (a cast member of *Blade to the Heat*) and it featured music of the Marco Rizzo Latin Jazz Quartet. I will never forget the way the excited audience members, primarily Cubans, rushed eagerly to their seats to hear the music. The whole room swayed with the rhythms of the quartet. Many people danced in their seats, and then they danced onstage!

At the end of the music performance, the cast of *Dancing on Her Knees* talked to the audience about what they could expect to see if they came to the play. I then directed the audience to the box office to purchase tickets. We sold forty tickets that afternoon! More importantly, we realized how valuable it was to link the "Free at Three" series to existing productions.

Respecting Native American Audiences

The Native American population is another important community that is often overlooked. Our interactions with the American Indian Community House (AICH), which is located across the street from The Public, included establishing mutual discount programs, attending their functions, offering group-rate tickets and opening up performance opportunities to their artists. We presented several Native American theatre companies in our "Free at Three" programs, and our literary department accepted scripts for possible readings, workshops or performances. Also, when we hosted our annual street fair, the AICH provided musicians and set up tables to promote their varied programs. One of the things I have learned is the importance of being sensitive to tribal identity. Lumping all Native American tribes together is similar to the tendency many people have to categorize all Asians together or all Latinos together, without bothering to understand cultural differences between Filipino, Japanese and Korean ethnicities or Puerto Rican, Nuyorican, Dominican and Cuban ethnicities.

A Telephone Call Launches Youth Outreach

Our youth initiative began as the result of a phone call in December 1993 from a Shakespeare teacher at LaGuardia High School for the Performing Arts. "My kids are falling asleep in class," Dr. Barbara Rowes said. "Can you help?"

We worked quickly with her to arrange a field trip for her class to attend The Public's current Shakespeare production, *Richard II*. Members of the cast spoke with her students after the performance. Dr. Rowes was so impressed with our quick response and interest in creating a partnership with her that over the next three years she brought more than 5,000 students to The Public to see an average of three shows per year.

Each student paid for his or her own ticket, because Dr. Rowes felt by doing so her students would develop a sense of ownership and a greater appreciation for the arts. We supported her by setting a discount ticket price that would affirm the value of the arts but remain within reach of a student budget. To make the tickets even more affordable, Dr. Rowes collected the money in installments and kept the tallies herself. (If she had not collected all of the money from her students before the deadline to purchase the tickets, she planned to make up the difference herself.) I can recall many afternoons when Dr. Rowes came to my office with a shopping cart full of rolled coins and rumpled dollar bills. It was the first time I had experienced such dedication on the part of a teacher to ensure that every one of her students got a ticket. Our box office reciprocated by accommodating Dr. Rowes's payment plan for her students.

After the first year, the students started to bring their parents. We did not increase the price for them. In this way, entire families could see shows with tickets costing $15 or $20 each, instead of the regular price of $30 or $40. We watched as the students were transformed from shy audience members to active constituents claiming The Public as their own hangout. They made friends with the house staff; several took internship positions at the theatre, working with our technical, production and administrative departments. They created their own points of entry and felt empowered to be in the building because of it. They also began to choose the plays they wanted to see. They collected money, which would serve as a deposit for their tickets. Playwrights or directors were dispatched to LaGuardia High School in advance of the productions to talk to the students. We would often hold post-performance discussions with the cast. The students then wrote term papers about the productions. They also were required to send thank-you letters to the cast, to my department and to George.

In addition to an increased source of income for the theatre through the students' ticket purchases, The Public received the less tangible benefits of a large amount of students enjoying Shakespeare and other productions, and in watching them develop a comfort with theatre-going, which would help transform them into the audiences of the future. We replicated this effort in different ways at other high schools, but without the commitment of an educator such as Dr. Rowes the results were not as successful.

Shakespeare in Central Park

"Shakespeare in the Park," a free Shakespeare summer series, is one of The Public's most popular and important programs—a true gift to the people of New York and the many visitors to the city. The Delacorte Theater, an open-air amphitheatre, was erected uptown in Central Park as The Public's permanent summertime home in 1962. Since then, free performances at the Delacorte during the months of June, July and August—including at least one Shakespeare production each season—have become one of New York's most beloved cultural traditions. "Shakespeare in the Park" productions are cast with some of today's most extraordinary stage and film actors, continuing Joseph Papp and George C. Wolfe's commitment to a multiracial, nontraditional American Shakespeare performance style. Each production regularly draws 80,000 people, all of whom see the plays for free.

In 1995, it became clear to me that we were not drawing people of color to the Delacorte, even though they were now coming downtown to The Public for performances. My department conducted an informal survey and discovered that the problem was not a lack of interest, but rather the ticket distribution system. Traditionally, if someone wanted a ticket to "Shakespeare in the Park," they had to stand in line in Central Park on the day of the performance. The free tickets were distributed on a first-come/first-serve basis. Lines formed early in the morning and the tickets were handed out only hours before the performance. It was an all-day affair. We found that many people of color did not have the flexibility to be able to stand in line all day to get tickets.

To help solve the problem, we identified cultural organizations in each of New York City's five boroughs and partnered with them to make tickets available in all the boroughs. The borough representatives attended the ticket distribution sites in their communities, greeting the audience on behalf of their boroughs and constituencies. Then we linked that outreach effort to a "Shakespeare in the Borough" initiative, which connected our outer borough audiences to The Public and to Central Park through additional borough performances in Brooklyn, Queens and the Bronx.

The Organic Nature of Group Sales

My staff and I knew that group sales would be an important component of our mission at The Public. However, we also knew that we would not be able to generate those sales by calling community groups that knew nothing about our work. They needed to get to know us, and we needed to get to know *them*. Based on my prior experience with DTH, I knew that in order for group sales campaigns to be successful, they must be organic—they must evolve through sustained relationships and community engagement.

In the pre-internet days of 1993, our primary source for lists of potential group leaders was the Yellow Pages. We used the directory to compile lists of ethnic cultural organizations, schools and universities, youth centers, churches, professional and social organizations and women's groups. We started with cold calls, introducing ourselves and requesting appointments to meet (at their convenience, at their address) and discuss possible partnerships. In our research into various communities, our first goal was to get to know who our target audience was and what was important to them.

Creating a list of groups to contact was the easy part. The challenge was finding the right person with whom to speak. When I called an organization, I introduced myself by saying, "Hi, I'm calling from The Public Theater. We have begun a new campaign called 'Cultural Explosions.' May I speak with the person in your organization who is most inclined to support arts, entertainment or education?" Once I got the name of a key person, I either called to set up a meeting or sent a letter, followed by a telephone call. This was very labor-intensive work, but slowly we began to get responses. Once we made contact, we invited these potential group leaders to our productions, and we encouraged them to bring their friends. Because at the time we did not have as much ethnic-based programming, we used the "Free at Three" events to cultivate their interest in the theatre.

Group sales is the strongest tool you have for generating and developing audiences, as well as for establishing a strong earned-income base. Inviting groups builds audiences in large numbers instead of one by one. They also can be nurtured to become "friends," donors or members of your arts organization. Additionally, when you have a steady, solid base of groups, you can give your funding sources or other potential supporters specific information about your audience. Group leaders also can become your focus group, helping to provide a sense of direction for future programming. You cannot spend enough time developing group support. I would like to share with you several examples of successful group sales efforts:

- The first production for which we made substantial group sales efforts was Eugene Lee's *East Texas Hot Links*, which was produced at The Public in February 1994. The play is set in a small black community in Texas during the 1950s, and explores relationships between the people in the community and segregation's impact on them. My department enlisted the support of the cast to participate in post-show receptions and discussions about the play. I hired an intern, a graduate student from Yale, Tiffany Ellis, who did an amazing job contacting a great variety of African American groups, helping us establish group leaders, and then making arrangements for the groups to attend the show and receptions. The positive response for tickets inspired us to set up several events in support of the show. We wanted to make sure our audience's first experience at The Public was warm and embracing, especially since it was in the middle of an extremely frigid winter. We pulled out all the stops! We invited several soul food restaurants (including Harlem's famous Sylvia's restaurant) to sell fried chicken and rib dinners during intermission and after the show on the weekends. We held a Valentine's Day singles cocktail hour in the lobby area. We encouraged groups to host receptions before and after the show. Consequently, there was an event after nearly every performance during the play's four-week run. The demand for tickets was ultimately so overwhelming that we extended the show for two weeks.
- Another great story with an accessible playwright and cast, *Everybody's Ruby*, by noted journalist and playwright Thulani Davis, is a fact-based drama about a largely forgotten episode in the life of the great author and anthropologist Zora Neale Hurston. The play explores the intersection of race, sex and

corruption when Hurston (who was played at The Public by Phylicia Rashad) investigates the murder trial of Ruby McCollum (played by Viola Davis), a black woman who shot a powerful white man in a small Florida town in 1952. The world premiere was directed by Kenny Leon and opened during the 1999 season.

For *Ruby* we held more than 11 performance-related events, which led to group sales of $46,000. There were pre- and post-performance receptions hosted by cultural and social organizations, and the cast could not have been more accommodating, including Phylicia Rashad (a stage actor who earned international fame for her work on TV's *The Cosby Show*). These events can be taxing on artists who have full schedules, but Rashad attended almost all of them. Experience has taught me that most actors prefer playing before diverse and curious audiences, and because we took the time to personally explain to the artistic team the value of their support in this regard, they joined in as much as possible.

• British playwright Martin McDonagh was already on his way to becoming an international sensation when The Public produced the American premiere of his play *The Cripple of Inishmaan* in 1998. Set in 1934 in a small village off the western coast of Ireland, the play looks at what happens to the residents (especially the title character, "Cripple Billy") when a Hollywood film director arrives to shoot the documentary *Man of Aran*.

The Irish community was one to which we had few existing connections. It was important that they learned about our production because it was specifically about life in rural Ireland, and the playwright had been acknowledged as a bright new voice that truly captured the culture and ethos of the Irish community. We contacted New York University's Glucksman Ireland House. They were so excited at the possibility of supporting promotional efforts for this play that they took complete ownership. They did mailings to their 3,000-person membership, hosted a panel discussion, and showed films about the island of Inishmaan at The Public. Their efforts were so successful that the show was extended twice.

There will be times when you don't have the answers—it is important to acknowledge this. In this case, we weren't connected to a prime demographic, but enlisting the appropriate resource proved invaluable.

- Similarly, several years later, I did a workshop for a gay organization called "The Gentlemen." They do fund-raising, focusing especially on African American events. One of the workshop participants said that the theatre community had never formally embraced the black, gay male community. So when we did a play that had the legacy of slavery and homosexuality as its central themes—*Insurrection: Holding History* by Robert O'Hara (a black, openly gay playwright)—this was the first group of people I called. The primary focus for this group sales effort became the one most reflected in the themes of the play.

- Loosely based on a true story, *Two Sisters and a Piano* is a lyrical drama about a novelist who, with her sister, is placed under house arrest in Cuba for writing a manifesto in opposition to the communist regime. Written by Nilo Cruz and directed by Loretta Greco, it opened at The Public in early 2000. This production marked the first time we created an events calendar that listed the full series of Public programs created in support of a particular show. The "menu," distributed in our lobby to various constituencies, included listings for "Free at Three"; information about our programs, including a reading in a local Spanish bookstore; a discussion at the Americas Society with a visual artist whose work was exhibited at The Public in conjunction with the play; and a pre-performance panel discussion with leading Latino playwrights (which was transcribed and later published in the Americas Society's quarterly journal). The calendar was an inexpensive but useful marketing and promotional tool.

- Jessica Hagedorn's novel, *Dogeaters*, was critically acclaimed when it was published in 1990 and was nominated for a

National Book Award. The story is told by multiple narrators, and the novel is a sprawling, fascinating look at Filipinos from different classes and circumstances.

Hagedorn, who was born in the Philippines, is best known for her fiction and poetry, but she trained in the theatre and had collaborated on many multimedia performance pieces, including several presented at The Public by Joseph Papp. She decided to adapt *Dogeaters* for the stage. The play, which features 15 actors playing 25 roles, was commissioned by La Jolla Playhouse in California, and had its world premiere there in 1998, directed by Michael Greif, with Alec Mapa leading the large cast. The production was scheduled for a run in February 2001 at The Public, with the same director and many of the same cast members. For The Public's production, Greif, Hagedorn and her collaborators (including playwright David Henry Hwang, author of the Tony-winning *M. Butterfly*, and dramaturg Shirley Fishman) worked to further transform *Dogeaters* by streamlining the narrative and focusing attention on the main group of characters.

Because of the play's large scale, we decided to present excerpts from it in a reading. New York University's Asian and Pacific American studies department co-sponsored this event and did all the promotion. The audience was largely made up of students, primarily Asian Americans.

By November 2000, we had confirmed the majority of areas for our audience outreach and had arranged the promotional events. We planned to promote the show both within the Asian community and to The Public's current supporters. The willingness of Jessica and the cast to participate in cultivation events was crucial, as was a co-sponsorship with a preeminent Asian organization that would help promote the show.

Before opening, we held a launch party for the show in Joe's Pub (an eclectic performance space adjacent to The Public, which is named for Joseph Papp, and features live music and theatrical performances) called "The Downtown

Vaudeville Extravaganza." This hysterically funny show was hosted by Alec Mapa (a virtuoso performer whose first break was *M. Butterfly*, and who played a drag queen in *Dogeaters*) and featured the production's talented cast. We primarily marketed to a Filipino audience, and the show—a paid event—sold out.

Another event, which we co-sponsored with the Asian American Writers' Workshop, was called "The Dog Eat Dog Party: Twenty Questions with Jessica Hagedorn." The Asian American Writers' Workshop, an educational resource for writers, readers and publishers of literature written by Americans of Asian descent, has become one of the most active community-based organizations in the United States. It is dedicated to the creation, development, publication and dissemination of Asian American literature. This celebration of Jessica's career was held at the Workshop, which promoted the event to its own membership and mailing list.

For *Dogeaters*, we also utilized our in-house program "Conversations with . . . ," in this case produced in association with PEN. This time the topic was "Portable Cultures, Global Identities," and the panel consisted of Kwame Anthony Appiah, Kelefa Sanneh, Coco Fusco, Jessica Hagedorn and Marin Roberts. We also engaged Jessica and Hill Harper (the only African American actor in the production) to do a reading at Barnes & Noble.

While doing research for the show, dramaturg Shirley Fishman utilized several photos by Marissa Roth from her recently published book, *Burning Heart: A Portrait of the Philippines* (to which Jessica Hagedorn had contributed text). We contacted Roth, and she allowed us to include an exhibit of her photos in our lobby. We displayed them for the run of the show. We sold copies of the book in the lobby.

We asked Joel Torre, a major Filipino actor who was featured in the play, to host the opening-night reception for the exhibition, and we included his recognizable name on posters placed in specific Filipino neighborhood video stores and restaurants.

All of these "invitations" to the community created different points of entry. We targeted students, young adults and parents, all of whom might be interested in the panoramic view of Filipino life presented in the play. We also relied heavily on grassroots advertising and distributed discount flyers in predominately Filipino neighborhoods. Many people who came to the pre-show events were not theatregoers, but they were very interested in the subject matter of the novel and play. We made the Filipino community feel welcome by creating numerous opportunities for them to "taste" the show before committing to buying tickets. Not only do people need choices, they also need a sense of security, especially if they are entering unfamiliar territory, and we tried to give them that.

This new audience came in groups—in fact, the largest number we had ever experienced from an Asian audience to date. Our box-office manager told me that people bought tickets in groups of six to ten, instead of the usual two. We also worked closely with several local Asian theatre companies who had ongoing relationships with actors in the production. We had been building partnerships with these groups over the five years prior to *Dogeaters*, in the 1990s, due to our realization that we weren't attracting Asian Americans to the theatre. Finally, when we had the product, the audience was ready.

The significance of the box office in a group sales initiative cannot be overstated. The Public's box-office staff was incredible throughout the *Dogeaters* effort (as they were with all productions). They were flexible and patient, often awaiting late payments for group contracts until days before the performance, because they knew we were building long-term relationships. The box-office figures for *Dogeaters* showed a gross income of $300,000, with 82% of all available tickets purchased. The show was extended twice, with 97% of tickets sold (700 tickets were purchased through a discount flyer promotion at $25 each). We booked in 40 groups over the course of the run, with the income generated from our community outreach department alone reaching a total of $60,000. We also saw a predominance of sales from New Jersey and Queens, two regions our research told us had large Filipino communities—a demographic that had not frequented The Public before.

This show also marked the first time we used the internet in a systematic fashion to tap college-age students, specifically those involved in Asian Pacific studies programs at local universities. I had two Filipino college interns working specifically on this show, and they were able to direct many of our event invitations and discount ticket offers via the internet, reaching hundreds of young Asian students and working professionals.

This was a gratifying production for us: we expanded our audience (our party guest list) tremendously. Attracting this new audience to The Public to see this single work, which spoke directly to their lives, was in itself a great success, yet our challenge would be to maintain these relationships, encouraging people who were drawn to *Dogeaters* because of its subject matter to see Shakespeare and other productions.

How to Incorporate Volunteers

As I've shown, volunteers and interns can be of critical importance in reaching out to new audiences. Even parents can be part of the process. One year, when my mom was visiting me for three weeks, I recruited her to solicit senior citizen partners. She became my "intern" and came into the office with me three days a week. At 73, and only recently retired, my mom had lots of energy and a tremendous passion for the arts. At the time, we had no listings for senior groups or centers. First, she went to the Yellow Pages and telephoned all the senior sites in each borough of New York. She would say something like this (and this was without any prompting from me, though I could certainly see where my marketing instincts came from): "Hello, my name is Theresia. I'm a senior citizen and I'm calling from The Public Theater. I would love to share with your education director some news about the wonderful programs being offered. We are planning a reception and I hope you can come . . ." As a result, we held a tour of the theatre and a reception (hosted by my mother) with bagels and coffee for approximately 50 recreation directors. Since my mother was a peer and one of the group, they trusted her. Her love of theatre and for The Public was contagious, and the group liked what they saw.

Of course, product is essential. When the community affairs department was first created, I had to work my programs around the season. What did I have to offer that reflected the diverse interests of our audiences? I solicited ideas from our partners so that we could provide tangential products of interest, even if what was being offered on the main stage did not directly speak to them.

One partnership that was (and continues to be) a tremendous asset was with Fred Powell, former chairman of the board of AUDELCO (Audience Development Committee), a 30-year-old organization dedicated to promoting the art and culture of African American theatre. AUDELCO hosts an annual gala affair at which awards are presented for blacks in the theatre. More importantly, the group's membership encompasses important tastemakers in theatre, and they are influential in creating a buzz in the community.

I first met Fred Powell, the owner of Barbara's Flower Shop in Brooklyn, when he provided the flowers to DTH. During a conversation, I invited him to one of DTH's performances. He and his group would soon become regular patrons. It was logical that Mr. Powell was one of the first people I contacted when I took the job at The Public. (He has continued to be an invaluable resource to me.) Mr. Powell offered to deliver promotional flyers and posters for The Public to all his clients on a weekly basis, free of charge. (These clients include 20 of the largest African American churches in Harlem and Brooklyn, and he works with several large, African American–owned catering companies.) I believe he did this initially because of the relationship of trust he and I had built over the years. But soon it was clear that he continued because of his own admiration for The Public: it is a place where he feels welcome and now brings large groups to productions several times a year. Not only did his delivery of the flyers save us time and money, but the advertising of the productions was so much more effective coming from him, a friend, than it would be coming directly from the theatre.

Another group leader, Mel Jackson, who lives in East Orange, NJ, has, since 1993, brought groups to at least three productions a year. He doesn't limit the choices to African American plays; he tries different productions, including one Shakespeare play. His group consists of neighborhood kids, family members and people from his church. He does research for each production and asks questions of the staff about its content. He then relays this information to his group before the performance. All he asks for in return is a signed poster by the cast. That's it. He is so passionate about exposing young audiences to theatre that even when he was having surgery, he made sure his groups were booked for performances. Once he saw a production that he hated, yet during our heated discussion about the play, he booked a group for an upcoming show. Because of the deep connection we had established with him, he recognized that he could still admire and appreciate the work we do and what we stand for, even if he does not always personally like a production. No one will love every single production, but everyone appreciates being treated consistently with respect.

Qualities to Incorporate

The Public's pool of group sales leaders had expanded so widely that the staff had to work with an outside agency to assist in the maintenance of the database and the day-to-day contracts.

Because customer service is critical in managing group sales, follow-up on all telephone inquiries is paramount; it is crucially important to stay in constant contact through direct mail reminders and by sending invitations to all special events.

I cannot overemphasize the importance of acknowledging the efforts of cultural partners. When The Public hosts thank-you receptions for group leaders, we do not merge them with other events or programs—we make all of our partners feel special. We contact group leaders regularly to make sure their experience with us was positive, and if it wasn't we see how we can improve it. We also send them a thank-you letter at the end of the year acknowledging their efforts, and we include a present, such as a T-shirt, cap, towel, CD or tote bag (inexpensive items that nevertheless convey sincere appreciation for their support).

The results of our work can sometimes be hard to quantify, but there can also be very tangible results: the efforts of group sales from the community affairs department of The Public averaged approximately $100,000 annually.

Collision of Cultures

All of the audience development initiatives have resulted in The Public's establishing solid, creative partnerships with more than 1,000 organizations and innumerable individuals within the New York, New Jersey and Connecticut (tri-state) area. As the word spread, many organizations were aggressive about initiating a partnership themselves.

We created partnerships with organizations established in their communities; the partnerships were mutually beneficial and yielded a multitude of programs. It was important not only to make contact with these partner organizations, but also to stay in touch. The personal relationships had to be nurtured.

The greatest lesson I learned while working at The Public is that successful audience development is a sustained effort. *It takes time.* We began working on these programs in 1993, but only started to really experience the fruits of our labor ten years later. People are now coming back to the theatre *on their own*, spontaneously, without the groups that first brought them to our front door.

Many of the events we created in the first ninety days have become the foundation of the department's work, and have continued to be fine-tuned as the department grows and tries to link the product to the audience. The "Open House," now a two-hour program, introduces the season through excerpts and panel discussions with the artists. *All* the departments at The Public contribute significantly toward making it a success, and that energy permeates through the building and out the doors. The demographics from our 2002 "Open House" truly represented George's vision when he first became producer—a "subway stop" of age, race and lifestyle. At this event there were students, traditional theatregoers and audiences from Latino, Asian American and African American communities. They want to sample the work, and they like being in an eclectic environment.

I am a strong advocate of audience development and partnership building: these are the most effective ways to develop a solid foundation, support our arts institutions and contribute to the building of a healthier community. Yes, audience development is a difficult job, but it will strengthen your institution and transform your community and audiences. You must be determined, focused and persistent. Keep going back. Keep talking to people. Everyone gets discouraged sometimes—especially artists. Lack of attendance can sometimes feel like rejection. But the audience may be waiting for a point of entry into your cultural institution—they may be waiting for an invitation to the party.

Chapter 6

CASE STUDY:
BRING IN 'DA NOISE,
BRING IN 'DA FUNK

Determine that the thing can and shall be done,
and then we shall find the way.

—Abraham Lincoln

My work for *Bring in 'Da Noise, Bring in 'Da Funk* represents the most successful experience I have had in engaging communities and bridging cultures for a cultural organization. The show was brilliant and the cast and creative team were eager to support our outreach initiatives and a profit was made. It was a privilege and an honor to have played an instrumental role in developing audiences for this show in New York and around the country.

It started with a vision. In a 1999 interview in the *Miami Herald*, George stated: "You know how New Yorkers are, they're *crazy* about the Knicks. I would sit there and people would be *screaming*, and I was just so jealous. I thought, I want to make something that will make people scream like that. I want to make them go: '*Unnnhh!*'—just go crazy." How George and his collaborators achieved that is the story of *Bring in 'Da Noise, Bring in 'Da Funk*.

The Public Theater's production of this original musical began with a summer workshop in 1995. Led by George and dancer/choreographer Savion Glover, with the help of researcher Shelby Jiggetts-Tivony, the artistic team began talking about African American history, culture and tap dancing, and how all these things might inform and intersect with each other. *Noise/Funk*, which is subtitled: "A Tap/Rap Discourse on the Staying Power of the Beat," tells the history of African Americans from the Middle Passage (the transporting of slaves from Africa to America) through life in the 1990s. The story was told through tap, music and spoken word, and was performed by professional artists and an incredibly talented group of young dancers.

When the show first opened at The Public in 1995, the goal of my department was to ensure the attendance of African American audiences. The show is fundamentally about our culture, and George wanted to make sure we were making substantial efforts to let people know that, and to invite them to see and enjoy it. We also wanted to make sure that The Public's members, subscribers and white audiences would see the production as well. We did not want to create an atmosphere that separated one group from another; we wanted to embrace everyone from the beginning.

Early on, while we were still in rehearsals, an interesting thing happened. A friend of mine directs a foundation that purchases prosthetic limbs for Yugoslavian orphans. They host a fund-raiser every Christmas, and the executive director felt they needed an event more creative and fun than their traditional annual auction. I suggested that the foundation hold a benefit around *Noise/Funk*. When my friend asked what the production was like, I replied, "I don't know, but George Wolfe is directing and Savion Glover is dancing. What more do you need to know?" Initially, my friend was uncertain; most of her colleagues were, as she put it, "very Upper East Side." The irony of the

Savion Glover in the Noise/Funk *production poster.*

conversation hit me—I was encouraging this woman to buy out the first three performances of *Noise/Funk* (performed by a group of tap-dancing black guys with dreadlocks), and her constituency never even came downtown! What a challenge! Because of her concerns, I had to really focus more heavily on her relationship with The Public. So we spent time together: she came to the theatre; she attended the Shakespeare in the Park production of *The Tempest*, featuring Patrick Stewart; she watched rehearsals; she spoke with George and his staff. We respected her important mission and made it clear that we wanted to work with her. She appreciated our care, concern and effort in making ours a fitting and mutual partnership. Finally, she was ready to claim the production. She identified individual celebrity sponsors to host each of the three nights and, after meeting with her staff and friends, agreed that this would be a creative and fun opportunity for raising money.

As a result, the first three performances were sold to the Princess Elizabeth of Yugoslavia Foundation for $250 per ticket, and audiences enjoyed a pre-performance dinner and post-performance reception with the cast. This created an enormous buzz and helped build a racially mixed audience from the beginning. Once we opened, with great word-of-mouth and stellar reviews, the show sold itself. When the decision was made to transfer the production to Broadway, we engaged in strategic planning about how to position it among various communities of color and people of different economic backgrounds. How could we make sure our audience development initiative would continue on the "Great White Way"? There were two basic concerns. First, we needed to create a bridge from The Public to Broadway. In 1995 there were not huge numbers of black people going to see Broadway productions. In my opinion, the two reasons were product and price—and I would venture to say product first, and then price. Second, our production, for which we still had ownership and responsibility, would be produced outside our home at The Public. We wanted to make sure it retained the vision and the mission of the producing entity. So what did we do?

Step 1: Reaching Our Audience

We took the product to the people. We took the dancers to all the boroughs of New York, where they performed in schools and talked to kids. We were the only performing arts group present at the Black Expo, where thousands of black people shop for new products. The dancers performed at educational fairs. The cast visited churches. In essence, we took *Noise/Funk* wherever there was a gathering of people, so that the product, the cast, the show, the concept was accessible to people in their own neighborhoods. Through the outreach, we were promoting the Broadway run, and needed to start to demystify Broadway. It became less "this place where I can't go" and more: "I want to be there and see this great show."

As one of the first and most important steps, I called the *New York Christian Times*, a local biweekly publication that is read by the black Christian community throughout the city. I spoke with the publisher, Reverend Dennis Dillon, who had seen the show at The Public and was interested in forming a partnership. There was an upcoming ministers conference hosted by Dillon and the *New York Christian Times* and, in exchange for The Public purchasing several ads (valued at approximately $5,000), I was able to speak to a captivated group of more than 200 ministers and promote the educational aspects of the show. Dillon also generously provided me with a booth at the conference.

The importance of developing relationships with the church community cannot be overstated. When you are making a connection with a church group, it is always a good idea to inquire about a dance or drama ministry. Almost all churches have a youth ministry, for instance. In addition, church leaders tend to be vibrant and active leaders of their communities. Through this connection, we helped make it possible for this very important constituency to take ownership of *Noise/Funk*.

Step 2: Access to Tickets for Students

A wonderful thing happened at a performance of *Noise/Funk* while the show was still running at The Public. Two retired school teachers came to see the show. They enjoyed the show so much that, the very next morning, they called me to discuss how to make sure that every black child in Brooklyn had the opportunity to see the production. (I always love a challenge!) Their vision became my vision: Find a way to provide tickets for all children—especially those ignored by traditional social programs—to see the show. Thus began my weekly meetings with Sister A'Aliyah Abdul Karim and her friend of 40 years, Elizabeth McKinney. Never in my experience had I seen such dedication to a production, especially by volunteers. During the four-month period between the closing of the show at The Public and the first preview performance on Broadway at the Ambassador Theatre, we met countless times in their Brooklyn apartments, doing grassroots networking and explaining the show to small groups of their friends who were business owners, educators and members of their religious organizations.

The three of us formed an organization called Griot Cultural Alliance, which gave a structure to our efforts. We met with superintendents of various school districts throughout Brooklyn to explore funding possibilities for student tickets. We solicited the help of several other individuals committed to this goal, and became an eager working group. I made sure they had all the promotional tools available to facilitate comfortable and abundant presentations.

The ticket price for students was $15. Often these women would approach local businesses to subsidize tickets for Brooklyn youth. They made it happen—not from sophisticated proposals, but by directly approaching businesses, schools and the children themselves. As a result, in the first three months of the Broadway run, Griot Cultural Alliance sent more than 5,000 kids to see *Noise/Funk* on Broadway, filling every Wednesday matinee.

I easily could have said to A'Aliyah and Elizabeth that it would be very difficult, if not impossible, to meet their ambitious goal, but by encouraging them to dream, follow their vision and have a sense of adventure, we were able to make the production accessible to young people who would not otherwise have been able to attend a Broadway production, much less one that reflected their own heritage and identity.

Step 3: Pricing

The Public did not have a history of charging our audiences $75 for tickets, the necessary cost of the show on Broadway, and we knew we'd have to address this. *Noise/Funk* was also one of the first shows on Broadway to offer a $20 rush ticket for the first two rows of seats for every performance, whether we were sold out or not. This allowed many students and tourists to see the show at an affordable price. We started to see large numbers of black teenagers sitting in orchestra seats on days when there were no group sales. They had purchased $75 tickets themselves, because they didn't want to take a chance on rush seats and wanted to sit up front—they saw *themselves* in *Noise/Funk* and were passionate about being there. I was able to obtain a regular allocation of seats (during selected performances) for audience development purposes, selling 200 tickets at $45 instead of the usual $75. I was insistent that these seats (available for groups of 15 or more) were located in the center orchestra, the best seats in the theatre. It is very important when you are building your audience that you do not put the groups that you're developing in the rear of the auditorium or in the balcony. You're better off not inviting them; the damage that is created by "second-class" status can sometimes be irreparable. (If you recall, the first experience black audiences had in the theatre at the turn of the twentieth century was sitting in the rear of the balcony next to the prostitutes.) If you spend tremendous energy telling an audience that they are wonderful, and you want them to be a part of what you are doing, yet then put them in the back of the house, how will they feel? You must be acutely sensitive to these situations. Your box office may not understand these things, so you will have to be a pricing advocate. I constantly checked to make sure audiences that received discount tickets were getting good seats. The benefit was that people would say: "Great show, great price and great seats!"

Step 4: Group Sales

During the interim period before the transfer to Broadway, I met with six black licensed group sales agents that worked in New York and handled Broadway shows. I needed to utilize their resources to market *Noise/Funk* to the black community, because it was impossible for my staff and me to reach all the groups we wanted and continue our work on the other Public Theater productions. I brought them into the planning process as soon as we made the decision to move to Broadway. This helped build a sense of loyalty and commitment. Their guidance had a major impact on the group sales of the show.

A $45 ticket price for group sales ($35 for seniors and student groups) seemed just right. This discount was promoted solely through word of mouth; there was no ad campaign or direct-mail effort. I had confidence in the potential of these group sales agents, especially when combined with our efforts in taking the product to the community and the efforts of Griot Cultural Alliance, which continued to sell group tickets, hold special events and promote *Noise/Funk* to schools until the show closed. A'Aliyah and Elizabeth became so adept at selling tickets that they both received their licenses as group sales agents and were able to broaden their offerings to include additional Broadway and Off-Broadway shows, generating added income for themselves. The most gratifying relationship is when everyone benefits from the partnership. What started out as a conversation about exposing black children to *Noise/Funk* ended up two years later as a successful business enterprise for them.

Step 5: Promotional Tools

Like the Griot Cultural Alliance, our efforts did not stop—could not stop—as the run continued. Word of mouth was a terrific bonus to our work, but we still needed effective marketing tools that would help demystify the show. We developed an eight-minute promotional video, narrated by the well-respected Phylicia Rashad, which contained footage from TV ads, talk shows, news programs, coverage from the 1996 Tony Awards (where *Noise/Funk* had received four awards, including best director and best choreographer) and footage from the production. It was a brilliant presentation that never failed to excite and engage its audiences. Copies of this video were made available to anyone involved in the audience development effort. It was used in small gatherings, schools, churches and in homes of group leaders to educate potential audience members.

Buttons with the show's logo were distributed to everyone at promotional events. Members of the orchestra gave them out, dancers gave them out—anyone helping to promote the show was given large quantities of buttons for distribution. We also made handheld fans similar to those used in many churches. We gave them out at every event—they were especially effective at the Black Expo, the Harlem Renaissance Festival and Harlem Week. For the show's tour, presenters

The cast and audience in Minneapolis.

would print their own venue and performance date on the fan. This enhanced the value of the product and helped to promote the show.

Through Sister A'Aliyah we were able to partner with a Muslim businessman, Bilal Muhammed, who had access to young men who could assist us in distributing flyers promoting the show. These personable, well-dressed young men thoroughly saturated black communities in Harlem and Brooklyn supporting our advertising efforts, special appearances and group sales. They went into grocery stores, barbershops and dry cleaners, as well as community and senior citizen centers. Because of his successful effort, Bilal went on to create a promotional business called Wise Up! and was hired to work on numerous Broadway shows and other cultural events. Remember: You can't do everything yourself, nor is it effective to do everything yourself. By partnering with local resources you increase visibility, ownership and success.

Step 6: Education

Since education is such a critical part of The Public's approach to audience development, we also created a brilliant study guide, compiled by Kimberly T. Flynn, which illustrated and educated readers about the genesis of the show and its creative process. It also provided questions for instructors, so that they could guide students to a deeper understanding of the work. At the time of *Noise/Funk*, students from LaGuardia High School for the Performing Arts were still working as interns at The Public. Kimberly formed them into an in-house focus group. As she crafted each section of the study guide, she would meet with the students asking them if it was clear, if the tone was engaging and if the material was interesting. Along with The Public's dramaturg, Shelby Jiggetts-Tivony, she embarked on substantial research to document the history of African Americans in tap and tap's historical development on a time line from slavery to the present. We were also able to include a sampler cassette of four songs from the show to be used with the study guide by the instructor. This study guide was not limited to high school students—it was written in such a way that it was helpful for adults as well. We produced hundreds of copies of the study guide and distributed it to anyone we came into contact with, whether or not they purchased a ticket. This proved to be another important demystifying tool in educating our audiences about the show.

The first year of sales for the show on Broadway exceeded our expectations: 96% of tickets were sold. The second year was nearly as strong: 90% of tickets were sold. All of the seeds we had successfully planted at the beginning were bearing fruit. In a television interview on BET, George and Broadway stars Lillias White and Heather Headley discussed why they felt black people didn't embrace Broadway. Affordable ticket prices was one reason, but lack of theatre training for blacks was another. Our effort for *Noise/Funk* was about selling tickets, of course, but it was also about changing the culture and providing an accessible experience where none had existed before. We had short-term *and* long-term goals, and both were important.

On the Road: The National Tour

In 1996, we decided to embark on a national tour, funded entirely by The Public, as a way to extend our mission throughout the country. Our board of directors consented to the tour only if we would continue our mandate to develop new audiences. George was interested in seeing diverse communities and, in particular, young audiences enjoy the show. My challenge was to implement this goal in an environment where there was no precedent for this type of marketing, and where there had been no sustained engagement to build audiences over time. George was quite clear: He told each presenter that the effort for audience development had to be made, and we would help support its implementation. Each presenter made a commitment to collaborate with us. This proved very important, because as I made calls to marketing directors, there was interest and a desire to help. I did not have to convince any of the presenters about the value of this initiative. They were ready. The tour was launched in September 1997, reaching 36 cities before it ended in May 1999.

Noise/Funk was not a "star vehicle," but it introduced phenomenal young talent. Where would the touring cast come from? The Public created a school (dubbed "Funk University") and auditioned tap dancers from around the country. Developing and training our own young dancers turned out to be valuable in many ways—it provided an entry point for their parents, whom I solicited to support our audience development efforts on the road. (No mother wants to see her child perform to an empty house.) They understood the importance of *Noise/Funk* and pledged to provide whatever resources they could. The mothers were invaluable—they constantly fed me names of groups, individuals and ideas to promote the show. "Funk University" had three sessions, and the company manager at the school, Monique Martin (who later became the outreach coordinator), implemented the activities on the tour. Monique was a natural to facilitate our activities because she knew many of the cast members from "Funk University" and she knew the show. She was an excellent spokesperson who could be creative and flexible from city to city.

At the start of the tour, I began to develop what would become a network of national cultural partners. I thought it would be helpful to get endorsements from national organizations so that as we entered each city we had letters of support encouraging local chapters to support the show. I worked with the following organizations:

- Girl Scouts: Letters were sent out to scout chapter leaders for each city we toured, encouraging girls to attend the show as part of their requirements for their badges in arts and culture.
- Coalition of 100 Black Women, the Links, Blacks in Government and the Urban League were encouraged to host fundraisers in support of "Bring in 'Da Kids" (see more detail about this program later in the chapter), one of our more important and satisfying programs.
- "First Friday," a networking event for black professionals, was held the first Friday (in some instances on Thursday) of the month. I attended meetings in Minneapolis, Denver and Boston where I was able to speak to crowds—sometimes totaling more

than 800 people—as well as give away tickets and collect names for follow-up mailings.

- *New York Christian Times* provided a letter of endorsement which we were able to send to local church communities.

In each city my first step for the touring performance was to contact the press and marketing department of the presenting venue in order to determine the quality of its relationship to the black community. The goal was to create a partnership between the presenter, the community and the production. An important step in this coordination was to hire a person (or find a volunteer) to head this effort. Some venues hired African Americans who had experience in the community to supervise the work and serve as the point person—this proved invaluable. Others used in-house staff, but relied heavily on advisors from the community. Once the point person was secured, we formed committees that focused on education initiatives, religious groups, social and professional associations, government employees, special events, promotional events and fund-raising. Each committee created and executed strategies to bring in new audiences.

A major challenge we faced on the road was familiarizing the tour cities with *Noise/Funk*—word of the successful New York show had not made its way around the country (at least not to the degree we had hoped). From the black community I heard, "What is it about? What does 'funk' mean?" The white community was afraid that the show was intended to make them feel guilty, thinking that it traced a history of white oppression of black people.

The committees needed to promote, saturate, partner and sell. This intense effort was a necessity because most of the time the presenter did not have an inroad into the black community. The initial conversations to promote *Noise/Funk* on tour opened the door to dialogue and inclusion. The results were significant increases between 10 and 20% in group and single-ticket sales, strong visibility of the product within the black community, and new bridges between the presenter and the community that could now be maintained with future events.

Next, we identified key community leaders to spearhead the committee efforts—respected leaders who were passionate about the importance of the arts. How did we find these leaders? First, we consulted the presenters. Then we contacted local black newspapers and asked the leading arts critic to refer key people who fit the profile. We found the influential churches and the respected educators and academicians. We needed all these participants to form a formidable team between 20 and 50 people. I made sure that the invitation to participate came from the presenters. I was positioning *them* as the cultural partners and *Noise/Funk* as the cultural product. The show had a mission: Bridge the gap between what's onstage and who gets to see it. I made sure that each presenter saw the show as an opportunity to make a difference. I urged them, whenever possible, to hire African American publicists to coordinate press relations or special events.

Next, we engaged a publicist for the tour. I worked with Kevin Gerstein, then partner in FourFront Press and Marketing. Kevin had a great relationship with the cast, having worked with them as a publicist in New York. Kevin knew many of the presenters from his prior work, which was helpful. He and I traveled to many cities together making presentations to each presenter's sales force, which included house, box-office, telemarketing, advertising, press and marketing staff. In our first meeting with each sales force, we outlined the goals of the production, the history of The Public and George's philosophy, and shared with them how we developed audiences for the show in New York. Once the tour got underway, we would elaborate on our experiences from different cities.

Another major component in each town was the kickoff event, usually scheduled between three and six months before the first performance. This event allowed us to gather together targeted advisory committee members and provide an opportunity to educate and excite potential audience members, ticket buyers and group leaders. These kickoff events were amazing. We hosted breakfasts, lunches and dinners, often with performances by local tap dancers and speeches by local black politicians. The most important thing we did was to empower each committee, each gathering of art enthusiasts, to claim the show and take total responsibility for marketing it to the black community. I realized the value of inviting people to the table—in each of the cities I visited, these gatherings marked the first time the leaders of the black community had been invited to sit with the marketing team for a Broadway show. The invitation alone encouraged their sincere participation. I was honest in my appeal—"This show will not be a success without your help"—and I defined success as having a large percentage of the black community in the house for every performance. My request to these leaders was that they help us design and implement the most effective strategies for reaching their community, and that they *sustain* their interest and involvement throughout the run of the production. This level of participation was very exciting to them; it gave them a sense of ownership, a sense of loyalty. It was immensely powerful to hear the response: "Wow! You mean I can help decide how you're going to position this show in my city?" We built our promotional and sales campaigns upon this loyalty.

In each city we created a specific structure. We set ticket goals, examined ticket prices, created special events. We designed a comprehensive series of events that provided exposure and interaction with the cast, which each committee could use in its promotional efforts. Helpful events included:

- Mini-performances by cast members performed for 15 to 20 minutes in community centers.
- Interactive workshops with bucket drummers were organized for 10 to 15 people. Our performers demonstrated on an elementary level how to play the pickle-barrel bucket drums. No advanced training was required. Who doesn't enjoy banging drums?
- Church appearances by a vocalist from the show. Vickilyn Reynolds, who comes from a strong Baptist tradition, played the role of 'Da Voice on tour. She loves to sing, so every Sunday in each of our tour cities, she sang in a church. We were able to track the sales from her church visits to the box office. One day in Minneapolis, we sold 700 tickets after one of her church visits.

- Panel discussions explored immigration, hip-hop, evolution of the beat, careers in the arts, etc.
- Tap workshops were taught by cast members. We brought shoes that the casts had outgrown and loaned them to any student who didn't have shoes for the workshop.
- Study guide presentations were given to youth groups by invited teachers or lecturers prior to the arrival of the company.
- Tap/hip-hop challenge contests for young people were held in the neighborhood. Prizes included tickets, CDs, T-shirts and the opportunity to meet the cast, who also served as judges.
- Visual arts and poetry contests were held: "What's Your Noise" or "Family Roots." Winners had their work published in local papers with their photo, and had the opportunity to meet members of the cast.
- Post-performance Q&A sessions were held. Cast members spoke for 15 minutes to groups of 40 or more following matinees or evening performances.

Taking advantage of events that were already happening within each city greatly helped to position the show. By the time the show arrived in each tour city, there was a "menu" already in place from which the community task force could choose. Empower the task forces to do advance promotion, then present the product to the community.

Bring in 'Da Kids

The local publicist in Washington, D.C., Alma Viator, framed this wonderful program. Very early on in the tour, she came up with the slogan "Bring in 'Da Kids." It became our mantra and a catchy slogan for the press to wrap their stories around. Essentially, it was an effort to provide underwriting for underserved children, enabling them to see a performance. The idea was simple: secure corporate underwriting for free tickets or those offered at heavily discounted prices to inner-city kids. Almost every city embraced this concept. Six of the

Cast members sign autographs in Minneapolis.

tour cities received grants of $5,000 each from the League of American Theaters and Producers to sponsor programs and underwrite tickets. A total of 33,000 kids attended outreach events outside of the performances, and 22,230 kids attended performances due to discount ticket programs. The community leaders on tour raised $125,000 specifically to underwrite tickets for kids.

Here is an overview of some of the wonderful activities initiated all around the country to develop audiences for the tour. There was a timeline for all branding events leading up to the engagement, as well as for building awareness and generating advance ticket sales. Each effort was different, each city was special and each initiative was amazing.

- *Los Angeles*: The company had a month-long engagement at Center Theatre Group's Ahmanson Theatre. The theatre hired a local special event planner to coordinate all *Noise/Funk* activities. The kickoff breakfast was held with 80 leaders of the black community in mid-January 1998. Carol Hall, a consultant hired by the Ahmanson, created a tote board, similar to what you see on telethons, on which each person was asked to pledge a number of tickets for inner-city kids. People made pledges based on their age, how many kids were in their Girl Scouts group, how many people were in their dance ministry at church, etc. By the time we went around the room, we had 2,000 kids underwritten by this newly formed committee. When word got out into the community, another 6,000 pledges came in. So, in total, 8,000 young people were able to see *Noise/Funk* for free in Los Angeles because of the work of this committee. This idea came from Carol, not me. I simply created the environment and, from that one breakfast, the community felt empowered to take charge.

In almost everything, there is a lesson for the future. Throughout the tour, we learned again and again how important it is to continually recreate the paradigm. You don't need permission from anyone to decide who can go see a performance. Simply claim it. The results will manifest themselves.

Subsequently we had a conversation with the group sales director, Peggy Bruen Delgado, who negotiated for us to get an allocation of seats at $10 per ticket. Peggy was amazingly clear on the importance of reaching audiences who did not have the kind of money the theatre usually charged for tickets. In addition, she bent the rules, allowing people to bring in payments layaway style: "Can I give you $10? I'll be back in a week with another $5." She allowed people that much flexibility because she understood the mission. Thanks to this internal partnership (as well as the community's commitment), the Los Angeles engagement was a financial triumph, and more than 8,000 kids were sponsored to see the show. Donations came from city officials, doctors, women's organizations, teachers, Mary Kay representatives, television personalities, police academies, moms and artists, etc. The run sold-out.

Not only was the number of tickets sold enormous, there were more sold for groups in L.A. than there had been for any other show we had done up to that point. This was in part because we created so many outreach events—weekly mini-performances, study guide presentations, panel discussions and shopping mall appearances. More importantly, the show would serve as a catalyst for permanent relationships between the presenters and the black community. That was the legacy the show left in each of the tour cities: learning how to initiate dialogue, relationships and partnerships. For these communities, *Noise/Funk* was only the beginning.

- *San Diego*: For the first time, 15 of the city's African American social and fraternal organizations, including the Links, Coalition of 100 Black Women, the Deltas and AKA (the latter two are large African American sororities), gathered together for a kickoff breakfast, and decided to collectively fund-raise, thus benefiting every organization. As a result of their combined efforts and the synthesis of their databases, they sponsored more than 700 children.

- *Portland, OR*: The community task force was headed by the commissioner of transportation, an African American, Mr. Atharee, who, along with his wife, had seen *Noise/Funk* on Broadway. When our presenter in Portland mentioned to him that the show was coming, Mr. Atharee offered to do anything to promote it. We formed a committee, which met weekly to forge relationships with youth-based organizations and promote group sales. The committee was able to sell tickets to several youth-based organizations as well as to adult associations, generating a healthy box-office income.

- *Seattle*: The presenter hired Vivian Phillips, a popular television host, as a spokesperson. She sponsored a luncheon where interested participants paid $30 for the opportunity to volunteer and work on the task force committee. The *Seattle Times* created an educational newsletter for kids and distributed throughout the city bookmarks with *Noise/Funk* info and black history trivia written on them. An innovative "What's Your Noise?" bus campaign featured art by local students, illustrating their own concepts of *Noise/Funk*.

- *Minneapolis*: The presenters partnered with Education Live to produce an extensive educational initiative. Members of the cast were flown out five months prior to the engagement to spend the day with a school that was adopted by the mayor, Sharon Sayles Belton. The entire school saw the cast in a mini-perform-ance followed by a Q&A session. The education committee cre-ated an abbreviated version of the study guide and held several sessions with elementary, junior high and high school teach-ers, guiding them on the best usage of the study guide.

  It was in Minneapolis that we held our first "Tap Challenge"—a citywide tap and hip-hop contest for kids ages 13 to 20, held in 4 different neighborhoods. The finals were held at the Mall of America, the largest mall in the country.

- *Chicago*: The Shubert Theatre and Nederlander Theatre were the presenters. I visited this city as often as I did (six times) not only because we had an extensive run there—four weeks in June of 1998, then returning for two more weeks in August of 1998—but also because it is my hometown and I was deter-mined to create history there. The Shubert Theatre developed a number of innovative projects to engage communities early in the promotional campaign. The first thing they did in January of '98 was adopt a class from NIA Middle School, located on the West Side of Chicago. They hired a tap teacher (upon my recommendation, from Najwa Dance Corps), arranged for a local store (Leo's Dancewear) to provide free tap shoes to the children, and the *Noise/Funk* study guide to the teacher who would be teaching them. By the time the children saw the show and met with the cast, they *were Noise/Funk*: They knew everything about it, had learned to tap-dance; they even owned their own pair of tap shoes. The teacher and principal were beside themselves.

  The Chicago presenters also created a task force that was responsible for education, special events and fund-raising. They sponsored a series of contests, including "Find Your Roots," which called upon local schools to encourage students to write essays about their ethnic heritage. The winning essays, with photographs of the kids and descriptions of their schools, were published in the *Daily Defender*, a weekly African American Chicago newspaper. The six winners won tickets to the show and dinner at a local restaurant.

The South Shore Cultural Center hosted a tap contest called "Create Your Own Noise." The Center held regional contests, semifinals and finals judged by local dance artists and cast members. The event was hosted by Bill Campbell, an Emmy Award–winning local newscaster on the ABC affiliate, WLS-TV. The media in Chicago was particularly supportive. Campbell hosted a half-hour special on his program "Chicagoing with Bill Campbell" about the outreach efforts for the show. It was shown several times, and would become a promotional tool to be used in other cities.

In Chicago, we also created events at shopping malls. We distributed flyers and buttons, and held raffles for tickets in the black community.

On one of my trips, three months before the first performance, we sponsored a booth at V-103's Expo for Today's Black Woman Expo, with the support of the *Chicago Tribune*, which offered free airline tickets and theatre tickets to *Noise/Funk* on Broadway. The booth was dazzling, with videos and posters, and the Shubert staff and I were able to speak to hundreds of people about the show.

- *Miami*: The presenters made extraordinary efforts to create different promotional avenues. They went to Barnes & Noble, where a local storyteller volunteered to talk (with use of our study guide) about *Noise/Funk* in the children's section of their five stores. In Miami, *Noise/Funk* was a win-win situation: economically, in terms of the diversity of the audience, and by virtue of the show's critical acclaim.

George commented in a *New York Times* Magazine interview ("The Man Who Would be Papp," Alex Witchel, November 8, 1998) that "we established local community ownership before the show arrived." As a result, the show recouped its investment three months earlier than projected, and had earned $5 million by the time of the interview.

- *Sacramento*: Numerous activities evolved from local support, including restaurants hosting dinners for the cast and bookstores forming into *Noise/Funk* centers for information within the black community.

The national tour was an enormous success because of the effort by presenters to relate to audiences they had never before reached in their communities. *Noise/Funk* created a bridge between each presenting organization and its African American audiences.

The "Bring in 'Da Kids" program was set up to attract and benefit young people. We sought out every group possible, including incarcerated juveniles, disabled children, children with AIDS, foster children, religious teens, Boy Scouts, choirs, dance schools, art centers, middle school children, college students and youth acting groups, etc. Early in the tour, my cousin's deaf Girl Scout troop came to see the show. We hired someone to sign interpret the performance. The girls enjoyed the show so much that we aggressively promoted the show to the deaf community in each subsequent city, hiring someone to sign interpret the performances when possible.

Each venue placed great emphasis on "Bring in 'Da Kids," which elevated tap as an art form and educated its audiences. The programs, including competitions and scholarships, garnered a lot of media coverage and ultimately drove ticket sales. Community leaders and educators were extraordinarily supportive because they understood the value of engaging young people and encouraging positive images for them. All these efforts were done for free or the cost of expenses.

The national tour received numerous awards and citations. I was honored in several cities specifically for my work in engaging young audiences for *Noise/Funk*. The impact of these audience development efforts is still being felt today. The groups, the partnerships and the collaborations we developed have been expanded into broader relationships. We created a prototype of how to engage communities and sustain those relationships by using the artist/production as the vehicle. Specifically, in our touring cities, marketing staffs appreciated the potential for incorporating our efforts into their marketing strategies. After *Noise/Funk*, some of them continued working with the consultants they had hired. By investing their resources, staff time and money in the promotion of *Noise/Funk*, not only did every presenting city realize additional earned income, they made new inroads into their communities.

Audience Development Summary in Brief

- 25 out of 36 cities created audience development committees to advise presenters.
- 19 out of 36 cities formed outreach committees specifically to develop African American audiences for the performances.
- In 15 cities, presenters hired audience development coordinators. Additionally, in 3 cities, prominent African Americans were used as honorary chairs (3 cities had African Americans already on staff who were placed in charge of this project).

Outreach Events in Brief

NATIONAL TOUR: SEPTEMBER 1997–1999

(these events are in addition to an 8 performance per week schedule)

MINI-PERFORMANCES	CHURCH VISITS	LECTURE DEMONSTRATIONS
53	20	11
PANEL DISCUSSIONS	WORKSHOPS	POST-PERFORMANCE DISCUSSIONS
5	15	50
VISUAL ARTS COMPETITIONS	ESSAY COMPETITIONS	TAP CONTESTS
3	5	8

Chapter 7

HARLEM SONG

It's the possibility of having a dream come true
that makes life interesting . . .

—PAULO COELHO
The Alchemist

Harlem Song was a production rooted in audience development from the start, from the creation of the piece through every aspect of its marketing and publicity campaigns.

In May 2001, I was invited to serve as audience development director and associate producer for the upcoming production of the new musical *Harlem Song*, conceived, written and directed by George C. Wolfe. Told through music, dance, film and photographs, the show was to be a history of Harlem's African American and Latino culture through the twentieth century. It was scheduled to open at the world-famous Apollo Theater in August 2002.

I saw this show as an opportunity to utilize all my experiences, ideas and wish lists for bringing communities together. First, I brought on board Marcia Pendleton (president of Walk Tall, Girl, Productions), whom I worked with on *Noise/Funk*. She had demonstrated creativity and dedication on tour, and I knew her skills would be perfect for the show. In September 2001 we held our first brain-trust meeting with the city's pioneer African American group sales agents, including Kojo Ade, Ida Epps, Debbie McIntyre, Mel Jackson, J. Seldon-Loach, Dwayne Trotman and Harlem Spirituals tour operator Muriel Samama. At this meeting, we realized that there were more than 150 collective years of experience in building African American audiences, and with our joint efforts we could *create* history.

We formed an advisory board to guide our strategy. All the members of this board had strong connections to the black community, and marketing/group sales experience. Equally important was that they were committed, smart and creative. Our goals:

- Form a task force charged with the responsibility of promoting and selling *Harlem Song*;
- Create an unprecedented level of multicultural awareness, involvement and patronage for the show;
- Maximize ticket sales by enlisting support from local organizations in fund-raising and audience development;
- Develop partnerships with the community, encouraging people who live and work in Harlem to invest time and resources in the production;
- Invite and engage individuals from Latino and African American communities to support, promote and sell tickets for *Harlem Song*.

We met monthly. We began each board meeting by generating ideas about how best to promote the show. We didn't yet have a script or cast (we knew George was writing and directing, and that was enough). All board members had seen George's previous work and that, combined with the history of the Apollo, was a winning formula. The landmark Apollo had launched many careers during its legendary amateur night performances, from Ella Fitzgerald to James

Brown to Lauryn Hill; it is also famous for its current *Showtime at the Apollo* television program. How could we lose?

We prepared a wish-list calendar of promotional events based solely on the opportunity to brand the name of the show. Because rehearsals would not begin for another year, we were, in essence, promoting and selling a show that didn't exist.

After six months of meetings and planning we decided to formally launch the audience development campaign. We planned an event featuring excerpts from the show. More than 1,000 beautiful and colorful invitations were sent to a carefully developed list prepared by the board, Marcia and myself. Harry Belafonte and Whoopi Goldberg served as honorary co-chairs of the audience development committee and as co-hosts for the evening. More than 400 people attended the launch event on April 11, 2002, at the popular Jimmy's Uptown in Harlem. It was a standing-room-only event with excellent food and an enthusiastic crowd.

That evening, the guests learned about the importance of Harlem from Harry Belafonte. George explained his vision for the show and introduced three performance excerpts. I explained the significance of the audience development committee and encouraged everyone to join a sub-committee. We had already created sub-committees, each to be headed by co-chairs, which would meet monthly: public relations, faith-based, special events, education, online promotions, lesbian and gay, and urban professionals. That night, more than 250 volunteers joined sub-committees. We distributed gift bags to each willing person.

Not long after this launch party, the sub-committee co-chairs contacted their volunteers, and committee meetings were scheduled. The outcome was amazing: each committee enthusiastically focused on creating and supporting events to promote *Harlem Song*. Each volunteer also served as the eyes of the community, identifying promotional opportunities for the show.

I want to highlight the efforts of the public relations committee in particular. Alicia Evans, a co-chair of the committee, prepared a community outreach plan: "Team Pulse," whose mission was to "offer a strategic grassroots outreach approach, targeting the African American and Latino communities, with campaign material sensitive to cultural nuances, themes and tactics." As a result of Alicia's great success, she was hired by the producers to supplement their press effort, ensuring that the show was reaching a multicultural community. Her committee set up numerous events, created and distributed flyers in the community and arranged for ticket giveaways. The committee was also successful in placing additional coverage in the African American press.

This committee's marketing and public relations effort was enhanced by the expertise of The Walton Group, a marketing firm hired by the producers. With their help, the committee made significant inroads in the Harlem community by contacting local businesses to support the production. They arranged restaurant discounts for ticket holders in exchange for advertising within restaurants (prominently featured posters, distributed flyers to customers, etc.), and pro-vided discount parking at the restaurants. All of these benefits were prominently listed on every promotional piece and in the program.

With *Harlem Song* we were not only determined to embrace the Harlem community, but, also, in order to consistently fill the 1,300-seat Apollo Theater, tap into and embrace the traditional Broadway community, many of whom had never been to see a Broadway-style production (let alone any production) in Harlem. We held focus groups consisting of traditional theatregoers and members of the Harlem community in order to help guide our advertising strategy. One of the comments consistently expressed in the focus groups was that the production needed to be an authentic story about Harlem, not the equivalent of a Broadway production—in other words, not a sanitized story of what people *think* Harlem is, but an authentic voice of the community's many experiences over more than seventy years.

Embracing that idea, we were careful to stress in the advertising that audiences could have a total Harlem experience by dining out and visiting one of the other cultural institutions in the neighbor-hood. Our advertising brochure contained a map of the partnering restaurants and other points of interest. To encourage those outside the local community to come uptown, Charlie Flateman, one of the show's executive producers, who was president and CEO of the Gray Line New York Sightseeing tours for fifteen years, arranged for Gray Line buses to pick up ticket buyers in Times Square and take them back after the show. We also hired a concierge to arrange for a car serv-ice prior to the performance.

A key effort in targeting the urban market was our pre-opening advertising campaign with black newspapers and radio stations. That was a major decision for a production of this magnitude: Not to focus all the ad dollars in traditional media sources. We felt that an advertis-ing presence in the black media, combined with our committee activ-ities, would help generate significant ticket sales.

Events and Promotions

Once the show began performances, the cast participated in many events for the traditional audience and for the purpose of audience development at a variety of venues, such as Sony Music's Atrium (a big lunchtime music crowd in Midtown Manhattan); Hue-Man Bookstore, the first major African American bookstore in Harlem; a DTH open house; the Bread and Roses 1199/SEIU theatre club; the Gay Men of African Descent 2002 gala awards program; and the Greater Harlem Chamber of Commerce's kickoff party for Harlem Week, which attracts more than 4,000 people to Gracie Mansion (the mayor's residence). The Greater Harlem Chamber of Commerce and the Upper Manhattan Empowerment Zone included flyers in all their mailings. We held booths at the Kwanzaa Festival, the Black Expo and the Baptists Ministers Conference. We invited radio personalities to attend *Harlem Song*, and they discussed their attendance on the air, (free advertising).

In the warm months, we distributed *Harlem Song* handheld fans to churches and local businesses. These fans were also given out at street fairs and weeklong festivals, as well as in select neighborhoods in New York and New Jersey.

The outreach to churches included a letter to ministers penned by the well-known actor, the late Ossie Davis. This was sent to more than 200 churches. Ads were placed in the *New York Christian Times*. Fraternities and sororities were also very generous in promoting the production to their membership.

We targeted Philadelphia and Washington, D.C., as part of our national effort to promote the show, and conducted on-air promotions there. We rented a booth at the National Baptist Ministers Conference, which helped us target the Philadelphia market. In Washington, D.C., we took a booth at the Congressional Black Caucus. We took advantage of numerous theatre-related cross-promotional opportunities with other multicultural productions.

Website/Email

We made the *Harlem Song* website as informative, educational and collaborative as possible. The producers and the web designer, David Risley, did a thorough job, providing links, history and the study guide. My team focused on the audience development section of the site. Early on in the campaign I met with members of the Harlem Strategic Cultural Collaboration, a member-based entity comprised of the largest and oldest Harlem arts organizations, including the Apollo Theater; Aaron Davis Hall; the Boys Choir and the Girls Choir of Harlem; DTH; Jazzmobile, Inc.; The Schomburg Center for Research in Black Culture; National Black Theatre; The Harlem School of the Arts and The Studio Museum in Harlem. Each organization identified a way to promote the production, because each recognized *Harlem Song*'s value to the community. In turn, we included links to each member organization on our website. We donated a dollar of every ticket sold to the HSCC to support the Harlem community. We were able to tie funding opportunities to the show and encourage early ticket purchases by letting buyers know that their funds would help support upcoming local activities.

A sincere effort was made to promote a broader cultural experience in addition to seeing the production. We included an extensive list of Harlem businesses and restaurants with menu descriptions and links. A potential ticket buyer could create a virtual Harlem experience through our website, choosing his/her transportation, reserving a table at a restaurant, visiting a museum, purchasing tickets to the show, etc. Several email blasts with ticket discounts were sent out regularly, targeting traditional theatregoers, African American patrons and lists compiled of attendees at other events where we made the show's presence known—thousands and thousands of names.

Education Outreach

The Department of Education in New York was extremely helpful in identifying school districts that would appreciate attending the show. A grant was set up to provide tickets to schoolchildren. These schools were chosen because of their students' high academic achievement. The tickets were distributed as a reward for excellent grades. We made our invaluable study guide available online.

Sales

Group sales were a substantial part of the audience development committee's efforts. They represented more than 15% of total ticket sales for the production. We contacted every group leader who had a relationship with The Public, and those who had seen George's prior productions. Advance sales for the show were 65%. The producers then encouraged sales by offering several discount packages, as well as deeper discounts for groups of 100 or more.

Various sales packages, including dinner, a soul-food brunch, walking tours, etc., were created and promoted online through Gray Line New York, Harlem Spirituals Gospel and Jazz Tours, and Harlem Heritage Tours.

Group Sales Agents

Licensed group sales agents (who receive commissions for sales they generate) are based all over the country and usually work on large touring productions and shows that generate substantial income. In New York, there are approximately ten licensed African American group sales agents who are recognized by the Broadway community and given various levels of access to Broadway productions. (Broadway yields the highest percentage of commission because of the volume and price of tickets sold, usually 10–15% of the price of the ticket.) I have worked with several of these pioneer individuals in New York and always strive to include them in the marketing of a production.

- Kojo Ade and Associates. Kojo is well known and highly respected in the community. He can always be counted on to have promotional material for African, African American and Caribbean events happening in the tristate area. He has an amazing ability to aggressively support the work he recommends, and for years has been a reliable endorser for the arts and cultural events in the black community.

- Ida Epps Turner. Ida has a particularly interesting history. She has been putting together theatre parties since 1972 with director Woodie King, Jr., founder of the New Federal Theatre. She opened the first black ticket agency in the country primarily, as she says, "Because white ticket office owners would not allow me to participate in the main selling effort. I was called in for the leftovers or for tickets limited to black productions only." Her strategy (which continues to this day) includes calling churches and asking the ministers to speak to their congregations from the pulpit. The message was clear: "We have to support black theatre." When she met the late Vivian Robinson of AUDELCO, who had a theatre party business, the two decided to work together in the promotion business. They created special events for matinees, which included dinner before or after the show, followed by a meet-and-greet with the cast; they held cast parties all over the city, bringing performers to churches in Harlem.

  For *Harlem Song*, Ida's dream was to open a downtown theatre party agency. She said: "I want a place where folks can plan parties with me, where I can train churchwomen to develop fund-raising events, and make black theatre famous by financially supporting it." The visibility of her work on *Harlem Song* made this dream come true. Ida now has a very successful theatre party business representing shows on and Off-Broadway.

- Voza Rivers. Voza is a successful theatre, music and event producer; founder of The Roger Furman Theater; and co-producer of *Sarafina!* and other South African plays. He stresses that many African American promoters are from the savvy recording industry and apply those marketing strategies to theatrical productions. He notes that the successful production of *Mama, I Want to Sing*, produced by Vy Higginsen, formalized this process. Her production of *Beauty Shop*, another very popular show, continued this formula.

It is also significant to look at the success of several touring productions of African American plays, sometimes referred to as the "chitlin circuit." According to Voza, these plays grew out of the church, which has a built-in audience and a permanent space. The chitlin plays carry a moral message while providing solid entertainment, usually gospel or rhythm and blues. Gradually, these plays began to attract larger and larger audiences, and churches needed to look for larger venues. Then concert promoters started to feature well-known performers, and began taking the plays into their mainstream concert circuits. A lot of venues, specifically in the South, were prime markets. The promoters used the same formula as they would to market concerts:

1. Spend 20% of the budget on marketing and promotion. There is no need to do more than this, because there is an extremely high rate of walk-up sales for blacks at the box office. There is not a lot of expectation for advance sales.
2. Make sure the message gets out. Use black radio stations. In major markets, look to black shows on TV and place ads with them.
3. Distribute posters and palmcards in large quantities (usually more than a hundred thousand). Distribute them everywhere, especially in churches. Focus on a built-in audience (the church community is an excellent example).

4. Cast the roles with recognizable performers. Even though former stars may not be as popular today as they once were, they still maintain good reputations; this carries weight, especially in the black community. Today, former stars often appear as headliners in chitlin plays and remain a big draw.

Results

After the show closed in December 2002 (4 months and 170 performances after opening), we had a wrap-up and thank-you meeting with the board members and committee co-chairs. At that meeting we discussed every stage of the campaign. There was a lot of excitement and pride in the room that morning. Everyone felt proud to have worked on a historic production and the first extended run of a theatrical production at the Apollo Theater. Charlie Flateman stated: "*Harlem Song* proved there is a desire in the market to have large-scale theatre in Harlem. The production laid the foundation with the efforts from the audience development initiative."

Harlem Song was not successful in a traditional for-profit model, but the production positioned the Apollo Theater as a major production house. *Harlem Song* changed the perception of Harlem residents; they now believed their community could sustain a major, long-term theatrical event with public interest and financial support. 147,000 of a potential 221,000 people came to see the show. Audience surveys told us that 65% of those attending were African American and mainly from a 30-mile radius. The first wave of audience members was from Harlem, and they were often repeat attendees. The second wave was from Brooklyn, another community with a concentration of African American residents. Our special events committee co-chair, Chantay Taylor, said that we might have sold even more tickets to Harlem and Brooklyn residents if we had opened another ticket outlet in each of those communities. Charlie noted that *Harlem Song* was more than a show, it was a community happening. Participating partner restaurants increased their business by 400%.

The biggest challenge we faced was getting white audiences up to Harlem. Prior to *Harlem Song*, there had not been an open-ended Broadway-style musical at the Apollo. The mainstream press at that time still profiled the criminal element rather than the rich cultural life of Harlem. It was suggested that if we had focused *Harlem Song* as an "American experience" rather than a "black" experience, the show might have felt more inclusive to non-black audiences.

For me, *Harlem Song* was an opportunity to stretch new muscles and open the door to new audiences. Immediately after the closing of *Harlem Song*, I was contacted to apply my experience to two additional theatrical runs at the Apollo: Salman Rushdie's *Midnight's Children* and *The Jackie Wilson Story*. We provided the Harlem community with a road map. Today it continues to be a thriving community for arts and culture, expanding upon these earlier efforts.

Chapter 8

AUDIENCE DEVELOPMENT IN THE MUSEUM FIELD

> To do Audience Development work takes will-
> ingness, creative thinking, planning, patience
> and resources—human, financial and artistic.
> It requires passion about the arts and audi-
> ences, and patience to being them together in
> meaningful ways.
>
> —ROMALYN EISENSTARK TILGHMAN,
> *"Audience Development: A Planning Toolbox for Partners,"*
> *Association of Performing Arts Presenters, 1994*

In the early 1970s, it was acknowledged by some museum directors that little was known about the typical casual museum visitor. In 1973, the Associated Councils of the Arts published a study, "Americans and the Arts," which measured participation in and attitudes about the arts based on a survey of 3,005 respondents. It stated that as of January 1973, over a 16-year period, 48% of adults in the

U.S. (or about 69.8 million Americans, out of a possible 145.5 million) had gone to an art museum. Education and place of residence were the key determinants of attendance: 37% of people in rural areas were non-attendees, as were 30% of those in cities with incomes under $5,000. The highest concentrations of frequent attendees were from the suburbs and cities. Interestingly, this survey noted that attendance did not vary by sex or race to the same degree that it did by other socio-economic factors. One reason cited for lack of attendance was the work schedules of visitors, which allowed them to visit only on weekends.

In 1975, the eminent child psychiatrist and Harvard professor Robert Coles published an article titled "The Art Museum and the Pressures of Society," through The American Assembly (*On Understanding Art Museums in America*, Columbia University, A Spectrum Book), in which he described taking one of his black patients to a museum. Dr. Coles and his patient went to Boston's Museum of Fine Arts and the Isabella Stewart Gardner Museum. The patient had never visited either place, and when he entered the lobby of the Gardner Museum, he asked, "How come they let us in here?" Dr. Coles explained that anyone could go to a museum. The young man did not enjoy the Gardner Museum and refused its future invitations. He did like the Museum of Fine Arts quite a lot, because of "the long corridors, large rooms and plenty of space for me to run and hide." Years later, this same young man, now married with a family, tried the Gardner again. He still found the museum unfulfilling and uninviting. He said, "It's not for me—for us—I was thinking when I took my boy there that this place, it's for people with money. I saw them marching some colored kids through, telling them to look here and there and everywhere. It was as if they were saying, 'See all you've been missing, here it is!'"

The mere existence of a cultural institution is not enough to engage every community. As discussed throughout this book, communities who traditionally have been excluded need to receive hand-tailored invitations that are positive, welcoming and sincere.

In his article, Dr. Coles examined efforts made by the Museum of Fine Arts to make visitors feel welcome. He noted that many museums had made successful efforts to attract underserved children and families: hours had been extended, exhibits had been geared to the interests of a broader public. (Remember, his article was written in 1975, well before what we might call "political correctness," or the raised consciousness that helped diversify the museum field in later decades.) However, he also described the experience of one young Italian boy who visited a museum with his family in the mid-'70s. This boy's father became annoyed at the way the security guard steadily watched them. The young boy later told his schoolteacher about their experience, and the teacher responded that although everyone "owns" the museums, if his father had complained about the guard nothing would have happened, but if someone wealthy were to complain, the guard would be fired. This young boy discovered firsthand that money and power had their effect *inside* as well as *outside* museum walls. The issue is not merely about money—it is about the whole matter of class and its various implications.

Dr. Coles suggested that unconventional and community-based outreach—such as satellite museums, mobile museums, art in public spaces and the presence of artistic "salesmen"—might break down the literal and figurative walls. The initiatives were helpful to support the thoughtful reveries of millions of people who might know nothing about art but wanted to feel and appreciate its impact.

Beginning in the mid-1990s, the museum industry began a field-wide effort to examine and enact strategies that could help build bridges between itself and the various communities it served. There is a wonderful document detailing these initiatives, published in 1998 by the Lila Wallace-Reader's Digest Fund, which has given millions of dollars to organizations across the country in the pursuit of developing new audiences. The Fund's "Opening the Door to the Entire Community: How Museums Are Using Permanent Collections to Engage Audiences" is a collection of articles highlighting success stories from various museums—The Art Institute of Chicago, Arizona's Heard Museum, Worcester Art Museum in Massachusetts, The Baltimore Museum of Art and The Newark Museum. It also includes a round-table discussion from museum leaders around the country.

In the publication, M. Christine DeVita, President of the Fund, notes that there has been a nationwide shift taking place in fine arts museums, spurred by a desire to serve all communities and make the arts a more meaningful presence in people's daily lives. The result is that a number of museums are taking steps to attract and engage a more diverse mix of visitors by using their permanent collections more creatively. Often the most severe handicap for those arts organizations who desire to effect change is the financial costs necessary to implement those strategies. To offset that difficulty, the Fund has supported these outreach efforts by providing millions of dollars to museums so that they may expand their roles in their communities. Ms. DeVita notes that through this initiative positive steps have been taken, such as the launching of innovative programming, the reorganization of collections to attract new visitors and the deepening of the museums' engagement with all their audiences. The new initiatives have touched everyone from boards to security staffs.

As reported in the study, the Worcester Art Museum, for example, learned that audience appreciation can help museums better understand the value of their collections. "Behind the scenes" tours are an excellent way to engage audiences. And when donors see more audience engagement, they give more generously. The museum expanded and diversified its audiences by re-installing and reinterpreting its collection of Greek and Roman art. As James Welu, Director of the Worcester, explains in the study, "The previous installation of the collection assumed visitors had a background in art history. We shifted the emphasis from aesthetics and connoisseurship to providing a social and economic context for the objects. This allows many more people to appreciate the collection."

In the roundtable discussion, Hugh M. Davies, Director of San Diego's Museum of Contemporary Art, makes the important point that "institutions gain credibility when they invite somebody with authority in the community to help create a program." He adds, "Museums have to make a conscious effort to climb down from the ivory tower and go to the audiences . . . We've helped people see a different side to us by opening a downtown space, changing our name and diversifying our membership and board of trustees."

Peter Marzio, Director of Houston's Museum of Fine Arts, describes how his institution "broadened our audiences by forming meaningful partnerships with libraries, churches, community centers and schools—always asking our partners to share costs, but never making that a requirement for working together."

In this sense, the strategies for the visual arts are quite similar to successful tools used in the performing arts. Every arts institution must be willing to share its premises, invite others in and disperse its power. It is also important for staff to go into the community and for the community to be invited into the institution, whether it is a theatre or a museum. Susana Torruella Leval, former Executive Director of New York's El Museo del Barrio, can cite as an example the success of her institution's participation on the local community board in the Bronx. She notes that El Museo worked "with the city to create bus routes and a visitor center to extend New York City's 'cultural corridor' beyond its better known boundaries, so that residents and tourists are more aware of and have greater access to the cultural opportunities that abound in our neighborhood."

Kathy Halbreich, Director of the Walker Art Center in Minneapolis, really articulates the foundation of all audience development work when she talks abut the holistic nature of how institutions need to approach these efforts. "Change can occur only when the commitment to do so pulses throughout the entire organization—from board to staff to committees," she says. "It's important for leaders to listen nondefensively, be open-minded and willing to challenge some of the traditional definitions of expertise to get the work done."

Independent of the Wallace Fund initiatives, several other museums around the country have made important inroads into community engagement as well. The Brooklyn Museum initiated a unique program several years ago. In a *New York Times* article ("Making It Work," Marcia Biederman, March 21, 1999), Museum Director Arnold L. Lehman advocates a previously heretical thought—"a little bit of shouting in museums is not a bad thing." The article describes the impact of Dr. Lehman's brainchild, "First Saturdays," "a free evening of music, dancing, art, film and general festivity" that made the museum a popular destination on the first Saturday of every month. Entirely community-based, this program is "an important part of Dr. Lehman's efforts to raise the museum's energy level and profile, as well as the diversity of its visitors," the article continues. The museum's increased attendance, while partly attributable to two major exhibitions, was also due in large part to people coming for "First Saturdays," then returning with their families and friends. According to the article, the purpose of the free monthly evenings, in Dr. Lehman's words, "is to make people comfortable in their relationship with the museum, to know that the museum is a welcoming place, a place that accommodates every age, every race, every level of interest."

Dr. Lehman also notes that the museum has always had a base of 20–30% of people of color attending its exhibits, but calls that "not good enough" in the multi-ethnic neighborhood in which the museum is based. Because the museum is located in a center of immigration, the goal is to soon reach 50% .

This kind of creativity and inclusivity is a '90s kind of attitude. Prior to this time, with some exceptions, museums really didn't care *who* was coming to the exhibits. As Dr. Coles asserted in his article in 1973, if people of color or other nontraditional audiences found their way in, they were rarely made to feel welcome—and more often made to feel that they didn't belong. There was an elitist attitude that became an incubator of exclusivity and exclusion. There was little marketing being done, much less audience development.

Recently, the Detroit Museum of Art has hired a community relations director who is making special efforts to embrace the large ethnic urban population. Other recent innovative measures include collaborations between more mainstream institutions and smaller, more ethnic-specific or nontraditional museums. One such partnership was described in "Ethnic Arts Groups Grab Spotlight, Big Venues Follow" (Miriam Kreinin Souccar, *Crain's New York Business,* July 28, 2003). In this case, audience development embraced two disparate museums. "El Museo is planning a major show—MoMA at El Museo—which will feature 130 major works from the Museum of Modern Art's Latin American collection, many of which have never been viewed by the public. The partnership with MoMA gives El Museo another chance to draw crowds and, significantly, the show gives MoMA an opportunity to get its name in front of a whole new audience." As ethnic arts organizations enjoy their new popularity, the author notes, the city's more established institutions see attracting minorities as the key to their own survival.

Today, the visual arts industry is taking active steps to bring together a group of professionals to engage in dialogue and action that address the gap in audiences and access. In 2000, the American Association of Museums board of directors established its "Museums and Community Initiative" to explore the potential for renewed, dynamic engagement between communities and museums. It is a broad-based, collaborative process consisting of national task force meetings and continuing conversations between community leaders and the museum field. In a working paper about the initiative, the association noted the following important questions addressed by the discussions:

- What is the museum's role in civic enterprise?
- What do communities and museums have to offer one another?
- How are museums pursuing the possibilities for engagement today, and what should they anticipate and work toward?
- What shared sense of purpose and values should shape and support the relationships between communities and museums?

As the working paper relays, the initiative began with the premise that "museums need sustained community interaction to invigorate their purposes and processes and open new possibilities for what museums can be. Communities will come to see museums as centers of community conversation, as places where a range of individual and collective experiences are welcomed and celebrated, as active participants in civic life . . . Rather than define 'community' for museums, this initiative will promote an expansive concept of community engagement consistent with increasingly blurred definitions of place and transcending the traditional implication that 'community' means a particular race, class or educational level." Consequently, the task force includes a broad range of community participants, from community organizers, philanthropists, academics and urban planners to leaders of youth organizations.

Museums, however—like individual artists and not-for-profit theatre in the late '80s and '90s—faced controversy, censorship and other freedom-of-expression issues as government funding became increasingly conservative. Today, the culture wars continue, but with a different spin. For example, in a *New York Times* article by Judith H. Dobrzynski ("Museums Gird for New Salvos in the Culture Wars," March 15, 2000), Joan E. Bertin, Executive Director of the National Coalition Against Censorship, notes that "the impulse to suppress difficult art and ideas is now coming from the left." Examples of this include feminists, civil rights advocates and gay activists; the article notes that "blacks have protested the art of Kara Walker, saying her often-brutal depictions of black life reinforce racial stereotypes. And some years ago blacks and other groups objected to a mocking portrait of Harold Washington, Chicago's first black mayor, in an exhibition there."

Museums are often lightning rods for controversy, censorship and other freedom-of-expression issues, whether as a result of increasingly conservative government funding or sensitivity from groups protesting what they see as work that reinforces negative stereotypes about race, gender or sexual preference. Even after the decline of the "culture wars" of the '80s and '90s, it can still be difficult to exhibit provocative art or art that is political—a critical point, since most contemporary art focuses on politics and social problems. Carol Becker, Dean of The School of The Art Institute of Chicago, adds that "the biggest problem for art and artists and contemporary art museums is the gap between what artists are interested in doing and what the public expects to see in an art museum." Curators and directors acknowledge that it is hard to know what might offend the public. The point, Ms. Becker says, is not to remove controversial art but to explain it.

ADAM HUSTED PHOTOGRAPHY

A "First Saturdays" event at the Brooklyn Museum.

Some museums take the position held by Maxwell L. Anderson, former Director of the Whitney: "Don't come to the museum if you're afraid of being offended, but we'll let you know in advance if there are works that are likely to be offensive." Awareness of these issues has to a certain extent put museums on the defensive. Is this the direction contemporary art is taking? What is the responsibility of museums and curators to the art and artists? How does cultivating an audience play into this?

Donna Sutton, Audience Development Specialist, joined the Metropolitan Museum of Art in 1998 to lead its newly created Multicultural Audience Development Initiative. This initiative works with several national multicultural organizations, inviting them to special exhibits (including one curated in conjunction with the production of *Harlem Song* that featured African American painters from the '40s and '50s) and programs (such as a concert of Puerto Rican guitar music, in collaboration with El Museo). Her department sponsors 20 programs annually targeting audiences of color, and her mailing list now has more than 8,000 names. One of the most positive trends of recent years is that a great number of museums have hired staff specifically to direct their audience development initiatives.

Let's take a look at interviews I conducted with several individuals who are leaders in the efforts for museums to engage new audiences:

RADIAH HARPER is Vice President of Education at the Brooklyn Museum. She was Director of Education and Programs at New York's Museum of African Art at the time of the interview. I met Radiah while exploring a cultural partnership with The Public.

DWK: What is the history of marketing of new audiences in the visual arts field?

RH: The museum business is young—only 100 years old. Until the '60s and '70s, museums were repositories for collectors' stuff, much of which was anthropological—someone who had money and time picking up fabulous objects on various continents. These private collections are at the hearts of the oldest museums in America—the Museum of Natural History and the Metropolitan Museum of Art, to name only two. The Margaret Meads of the world and various other scholars worked with different ethnic groups and convinced cultures to give them their sacred objects. Other times, they stole, sold or bartered from these cultural groups.

If you are fund-raising, it's not about a collector's haven— it's about access. Early on, museums didn't care how many people came. Then in the '70s and '80s, they had to look to government funding sources for support. Because of this, they were required to state who would benefit from their collections, which necessitated ads, flyers, direct mail and networking with organized groups. Some museums became smart and specialized. We experienced the growth of children's museums, history museums and science museums. It allowed them to target audiences and focus marketing efforts. In the '80s, museums realized the world was more than white, and it became a multicultural conversation, also pushed by the need for government dollars. Museums began to ask themselves, "How do we engage communities of people who aren't coming? How do we define our audience?"

To develop audiences, museums first need to come to terms with the concept of audience development and realize that it is fundable. "New audiences" is a code for "people of color." Someone in senior management has to keep the fire lit until this initiative is institutionalized. Often they are not wholly successful because there is rarely someone of color in a position to maintain these strategies. It is hard to discuss these concepts without someone in a decision-making position who reflects these communities. Museums have to define a new audience, another language, and let these issues be part of conversations.

DWK: Who has the most progressive programs in museums?

RH: The Anacostia Museum in southeast Washington, D.C., reaches its community. Years ago in the '80s, they had a director, John Kinard, a lion in the field who understood the value of engaging the local community. They did an exhibit on roaches! And people came. That is being *in* the community. Kimberly Camp at the Smithsonian Museum runs their experimental gallery—a hole-in-the-wall space in the middle of the castle. She has done interesting things to reach black audiences. For instance, she did an exhibition on homelessness: You walked through the exhibit and were *forced* to move into certain spaces. One space was a morgue and you could lie in the drawer. Another space was an elevator in the projects where you could smell urine. At the end of the exhibit, visitors wanted to *do something*. There was a suggestion board and books at the end of the exhibit.

DWK: What is the Museum of African Art doing?

RH: I am very proud of who comes to programs at the Museum of African Art. I have been in the field long enough to hear that "blacks don't come to museums." But they come here because of what we offer, such as art workshops. I talk to every artist who participates and stress the importance of interacting with the audience and combining that experience with their artistry. Something happens. It becomes a platform for visitors to have an "aha" experience that there is a culture and history of African people.

There are few marketing dollars, so we spend more time with networking, collaborations and reaching out to African populations and online resources. We are trying to be savvy and position ourselves with smart urban media sources. We have a program called "Third Thursday"—free admission after-hours, with live music. Essentially, we encourage people to use the museum for networking events—close to 200 people come for these evenings. This is an example of effective marketing. It is not an educational event and it is different from a program—its function is to get people in the door.

DWK: What is your vision for museum audiences?

RH: I wouldn't race to build attendance, race to the bottom line. I would like to see more time spent collaborating with other institutions, and with artists, doing significant programming that could be marketed. I would build programs that have lasting impact, that emphasize lifelong learning, and are more than just a tour. We need to encourage more repetition and repeat visitation so that, through our programs, museums are not seen as elitist places but places to visit regularly. Museums should become more alive in people's lives. Art is a tool for healing. With all the troubles schools are having, it seems to be a great place to build confidence and self esteem. I would like to see more collaboration with schools and museums, so we serve people in ways that will affect their lives.

DONNA SUTTON at the Metropolitan Museum of Art elaborates on her role as a diversity specialist. Donna and I have served on several panels together, and she is a great lecturer for all my NYU marketing classes. I admire her energy and vision as she pioneers diversity initiatives at the Met.

DWK: Why do you think audience development is important?

DS: It is very important to educate and inspire. At the Met, my goal is to increase exposure for our numerous collections. We have a multicultural collection already, and a lot of people don't know it. My job is to make them aware and see how they are represented. So when you come, you are not only educated but also inspired. When you see yourself reflected on the wall, it adds to your sense of dignity. But awareness is not enough; people must participate in programs and activities. It's not one-sided. It's the museum's responsibility to learn and understand their needs. I feel very fortunate to be at the museum; we are on the right track. It's incredible what happens when we get together.

DWK: What is the museum doing?

DS: The advisory committee, which is comprised of leaders of cultural and social organizations, meets twice a year. We are just at the beginning. Even though I am the audience development specialist, it is important to have an advisory committee to develop partnerships, understanding and trust. When you develop the trust, all kinds of doors open up. Currently we accomplish our goals through receptions, tours and talks. Initially our efforts are focused on ethnicity. When we launched the initiative, we felt it necessary to separate each group to understand its needs and issues, so the museum could figure out what it needed.

My mission statement lists our goals as follows: to increase awareness of the museum's programs and collections, to create ongoing relationships with the many diverse communities that make up New York, to diversify museum visitorship and membership, and to increase participation in the museum's activities.

DWK: Who are your communities?

DS: All communities. Living in New York City, we are fortunate to have so many—African American, Latino, Asian, young, older and physically challenged. We enjoy diversity in its broadest sense. In the beginning we concentrated on ethnic groups, but the effort is not limited to just race; it is also age-centered and for the physically challenged. Here at the Met, we have receptions, tours, gallery talks and lectures inspired by our multicultural collection. I also feel it is important to support and participate in cultural and civic events in New York. For example, we have a daily "Hour of Solace" where different instrumentalists and choruses come and sing, and people can reflect and hope.

We also have collaborative efforts with different institutions, including The Studio Museum in Harlem and El Museo del Barrio. Last year we had a Yoruba beading show. Our curator talked about the collection, and we hired buses to take people to SMH and see their collection. It was very successful and we plan a similar collaboration this winter. We have a presence at the Asian American Heritage Awards and with the New York Coalition of 100 Black Women, which hosts a role model program, mentoring young girls. We also host a youth summit with the National Conference of Artists, which explores careers in the art world for African Americans.

We also strengthen our efforts through the media. We are expanding our initiative with community papers, radio and television through advertising, press releases and media alerts. A multicultural newsletter was developed as a communication vehicle. I would like to see us even more involved with community papers and newsletters—essentially bringing in the media as a tool of communication.

DWK: In a perfect world what is your vision for how audiences can be engaged?

DS: That our visitors will feel at home, without any reservation. With the participation of different communities, it would be such a mix of people that you could look in the Great Hall and see everyone represented and know they are at home. By continuing this initiative, we know we will make it happen. The trustees and all the staff support the Met's initiative, which is very important. It's impossible to have success without support from the top. The trustees at the Met are on the committees as well. They hear concerns and immediately work to remedy those concerns.

Deborah Starling Pollard discusses her work as Community Liaison at Pittsburgh's Carnegie Museum of Art.

DWK: Why was your position created at Carnegie?

DSP: They brought in a market researcher and found out they were not reaching the underserved population of Pittsburgh. The zip codes were in the upper echelon and the visitors to the museum were mostly white. Through the Pittsburgh Foundation and Regional Asset Board it was mandated that Carnegie had to get someone to create more of a balance. There was also a financial incentive—to get the 10% for cultural entertainment dollars administered by the city. They interviewed more than 30 people for the job. Pat Mitchell, Executive Director of the now-defunct Kuumba Trust, recommended me, and I was hired in November '99. There was no structure to the position when I began. I created a survey and went into the community and spoke to black and Latino organizations to find out their perception of the museum. They said they felt extremely disconnected from cultural institutions like the museum, especially feeling underrepresented in works of art in the galleries. "There is no one who looks likes me." Latinos felt they were not represented at all. Picasso is claimed by Europeans as French, not Spanish, so there is no mirror. As a result, they had no desire to be members of the museum. I reported this back to the museum exactly as they reported it to me.

In order to address the real concerns in the community, black folks asked for a step-by-step integration of underserved communities into the museum. I came up with a proposal called "Stepping Stones," which is particularly geared toward family-oriented communities, including Latinos. We are identifying families who are interested in art and would like to participate with no barriers—we provide each family with yearly memberships. But if you just give a membership, people may or may not come. To really integrate the community, I also suggest having quarterly visits where families can participate in existing programs and explore works of art in the gallery. The space should look different each time they come. This is a three-year program for the first 100 families—each year there will be a new group of 100 families.

We do have culturally focused programming now, such as the art and music programming for Latin American Heritage Month, a collaboration with the Museum of Natural History, which we held in the fall of 2000. We increased attendance by 1,000 with that investment, which showed unity and helped bond both our museums' efforts together. This sealed it for the Latino community and began an ongoing dialogue. Now I can offer programming because there is a relationship instead of the usual once-a-year hit.

Our audience development initiatives also reach multigenerational audiences and seniors. My dream is to have flourishing programs—and seniors need affordable prices. One of my initiatives, "Senior Spotlight," brings in seniors for lunch and tours and lively discussions about art with the docents. Initially, some of the docents assumed that African American seniors are not knowledgeable about art. They have found that the seniors are a repository of information and will eagerly share their information. The price is $20, but I subsidize those in need for $10. I want the price to be $10 always. I hope the museum will recognize the value of this program and offer this premium across the board. Ideally, the program will be incorporated into the museum's main marketing and education efforts and not be funded by my budget. It needs to be a sustained effort and institutionalized, not something that will disappear if I leave.

SANDRA JACKSON, Director of Education and Programs at The Studio Museum in Harlem, collaborated with me to combine our audiences in June 2001, when The Public brought actors Don Cheadle and Jeffrey Wright up to the museum with playwright Suzan-Lori

Parks to discuss its production of *Topdog/Underdog*. The discussion had a standing-room-only audience of approximately 200 people of all ages, predominately African American. One audience member, Isisara Bey, Vice President for Corporate Affairs at Sony BMG Music, was so inspired by the discussion that she immediately purchased 100 tickets for her employees.

DWK: What is your experience with developing audiences for the visual arts?

SJ: My desire, instinct and drive came from home. I have always been very interested in accessibility. I have worked at several organizations, including a gallery at Sonoma State University called the Intercultural Center, which helped engage diverse populations to learn more about their own culture and disseminate their ideas. Our population at Sonoma State included African Americans, Mexicans and Asian Pacific Islanders, and our work was done through student activities. This was my first adult experience planting seeds and being involved in community work, accessibility and building levels of awareness. As a child I saw people organizing in communities, placing ads in church bulletins, but larger organizations have moved away from this kind of grassroots marketing.

I went to graduate school and continued to do work in the visual arts and with community arts organizations, which empower people by connecting them to cultural history. In college I was connected to student populations and programs that were more theme-based. I learned how to curate not just exhibitions but also programs. Then I moved to New York and became involved in a theoretical program at the Whitney Museum. While there I was in a curatorial role, and I realized that making information accessible depends on asking critical questions: Is your institution visitor-centered? What makes and breaks the visitor's experience? Has your institution invested in staff to improve the visitor's experience? Does your institution value audience input?

I want to stress the importance of language and materials. I was at the Whitney to develop an intergenerational program, and that's when I started working differently, understanding that people respond to people, not paper. People respond to their own individual connections to things, not a prescribed idea. The program I ran dealt with seniors, families, adults and youths. There was a different dynamic for each one. It dealt with class. I started talking to people and went to organizations asking them what their needs were. As a result of what I learned I launched a campaign for myself, doing informational interviews for the 11 organizations funded by The Pew Charitable Trusts.

DWK: Why do you think audience development is important?

SJ: Because people need to know what resources and accessibility they have. This leads to knowledge, self-empowerment and awareness.

DWK: What is The Studio Museum doing?

SJ: Last year, we worked on building resources. What we are doing now is working to bring into leadership positions people who are well trained and willing to go the extra mile. We also make sure there is a local voice in the community and have developed a community advisory group. This helps create a public image for the museum. The advisory committee consists of local community leaders, such as employees of Harlem Hospital, the Schomburg Center for Research in Black Culture, Harlem School of the Arts, High 5 [an access organization that offers young people tickets to arts events for only five dollars], United Neighborhood Housing of New York, all of whom are interested in using cultural resources that have a broad reach for their constituents.

Museums need to get back to looking at themselves as public institutions and service organizations. Simultaneously, we should create equity between our approach towards community-based activities and academic institutional recognition in the greater art world. I started this process by holding informational meetings with as many cultural organizations as possible. I now hold events with these partners serving as co-hosts; for example,

Black Diamonds, a socially mobile group of black entrepreneurs, works with me on a program called "Uptown Friday," which consists of music and light refreshments. When we began in December 2000, 75 people came; now there are several thousand attendees. The next step with this group of 800 is to persuade them to join the "Friends of the Museum" and become donors to the museum. We now have 200 members with 10 to 15 joining per month.

I recognize how difficult it is to begin this process, but you start with your friends first, and then expand to the immediate neighborhood, enabling others to become your mouthpiece. When I was at the Whitney Museum, I would not stand on 5th Avenue handing out flyers, but in Harlem it is quite common and effective to distribute flyers, free passes or balloons on the street.

DWK: What would you like to see happen?

SJ: I love George Wolfe's idea of theatre being a subway stop. I would love for the museum to invest in creating media and other public information that reaches diverse audiences in a way that makes them feel it is something they need and is crucial to their environment. There are some parents who don't know they can go to the library. I would like to continue building alliances with The Public Theater, Harlem Hospital and other organizations that are not just art-oriented, but can have reciprocal benefits and are noncompetitive.

DWK: In a perfect world what is your vision for how audiences can be engaged?

SJ: They should be actively engaged through interaction and an exchange of ideas between those presenting and facilitating and the audience. People learn more when there is a physical or verbal exchange. There needs to be a "buy-in," some sort of investment. People should own the space they are coming to and know that there is something there for them.

We had a focus group recently, to learn what people felt about us and how we were perceived—are we just a "black museum"? We found out that people are not aware of us. That's what audience development is—relating information and building a sustainable relationship so people feel invited, engaged, challenged, welcomed, able to get something and give something.

Can we go too far in this effort to diversify museum-goers? In a *New York Times* article ("Memo to Art Museums: Don't Give Up on Art," December 3, 2000), critic Roberta Smith argues that some exhibitions look like "historical society displays. More and more they are in danger of becoming places where larger social and historical patterns are either consciously or unconsciously played out, where people of all ages are given cursory lessons in history and morality," noting that museums are driven by other needs—including financial security, popular acclaim or social relevance—more than the desire to showcase art. As a case in point, Ms. Smith criticizes a recent hip-hop exhibition at the Brooklyn Museum titled "Hip-Hop Nation: Roots, Rhymes and Rage," describing it as "an exhibition that veers between product showroom and up-to-the-moment historical society, with little in the way of art in between." She suggests that the hip-hop show could have been much improved had it not pandered so clearly and narrowly to those who are already fans of the music. If the exhibit had been more traditional, she adds, and appropriate to a serious museum setting, it would have appealed to a broader audience and been more representative of the actual achievements of hip-hop.

Other experts, however, don't think we've gone for enough. In "Audience, Ownership and Authority: Designing Relations between Museums and Communities" (*Museums and Communities: The Politics of Public Culture*, Smithsonian Institution Press, Washington, D.C., 1992), author Steven D. Lavine notes that "many efforts to diversify museums have been modest to date. Large-scale social and demographic changes in industrial societies generally and the United States specifically will inevitably mean that museums will be asked to alter their programming to accommodate more diverse constituencies . . . Further institutional change is inevitable. Since the civil rights and war protest movements of the '60s and '70s, every institution that is seen to hold power (whether it be cultural, educational or governmental), has been open to question. This means that exhibitions will be subjected to searching examinations for social, cultural, political or sexual commitments. As the demographics of the U.S. population continue to shift and we move toward being a society in which the majority of the population will belong to minority groups, we can expect these external pressures to grow."

Lavine feels the best innovations in a museum's relationship with its community are evident in children's museums, history museums, and ethnic- and community-based museums. For larger museums, audience research is important for achieving community input.

In preparing for its limited move to Queens, New York's Museum of Modern Art crafted an audience development initiative to engage the multicultural community. At the Metropolitan Museum of Art, there are 3,000 employees and more than 5 million visitors per year. The other museums discussed in this chapter are much smaller. SMH has a membership of 1,000. However, the goals they all have for audience development are virtually the same. It's interesting to note, however, that while the Met is trying to develop audiences of color— primarily black, Latino and Asian—SMH is trying to develop white audiences. In both cases, the objective is to make the museum, and its art, accessible and open to everyone.

Chapter 9

THE FUTURE

You must be the change you wish to see
in the world.
                    —Mohandas Gandhi

The hip-hop movement and its influence on our culture are of
great interest to me. I think the dance, theatre and museum fields
may benefit from studying this art form, which has grown to tremendously impact fashion, merchandising, film and entertainment. Hip-
hop has pervaded the performing and visual arts and is one of today's
most successful art forms, crossing barriers of race, age, class and geography. How is this useful in understanding the application of audience
development? I believe there is something to be learned from the phenomenal success of this $10 billion industry. How has it maintained
the purity of its sound without comprising its art?

How did rap go from underground club music to experience the
immense popularity it now enjoys with whites? Neil Strauss notes in a
New York Times article ("The Hip-Hop Nation: Whose Is It? A Land

with Rhythm and Beats for All," August 22, 1999) that "white people are listening to and using elements of rap not for theft (as was done in minstrelsy) but because they relate to it, because the music is a legitimate part of their cultural heritage."

He adds that "hip-hop is the ultimate capitalist tool. Clothing companies taking advantage of the music's popularity first became evident in *Source* and *Vibe*. The style evoked by hip-hop was a source of money making." This was evident in the recent exhibit on hip-hop at the Brooklyn Museum and is equally apparent in products bearing designer labels such as Gucci, Chanel, Ralph Lauren and Tommy Hilfiger. In 1996, Hilfiger was the number one apparel company traded on the New York Stock Exchange, due primarily to his embrace of hip-hop and the large suburban audience excited by that urban-prep look.

Hip-hop has become one of the most influential forces in American culture. This was recognized in a two-day "summit" held in June 2001 in New York, where a disparate group of more than 300 musicians, politicians, music executives and religious leaders came together to examine hip-hop's impact. Nation of Islam leader Louis Farrakhan urged artists to take a leadership role in the black community by uplifting and guiding the younger generation. Through his leadership, artists developed an expansion program, forming an alliance with the National Association for the Advancement of Colored People, the Southern Christian Leadership Conference, the Million Family Movement and the Nation of Islam.

Hip-hop arrived on Broadway in November 2002 with *Russell Simmons Def Poetry Jam on Broadway*. Marcia Pendleton and I were responsible for audience development after the opening of the show, which *New York Times* critic Ben Brantley called: "The most singular offering in mainstream New York theatre these days." This show was able to attract a multicultural audience and a younger demographic. It ran for six months and won a 2003 Tony for best special theatrical event.

What is the connection between hip-hop and the idea of developing audiences, building bridges to communities? I believe the parallel is quite simple: The arts, performing and visual, feed the soul; they

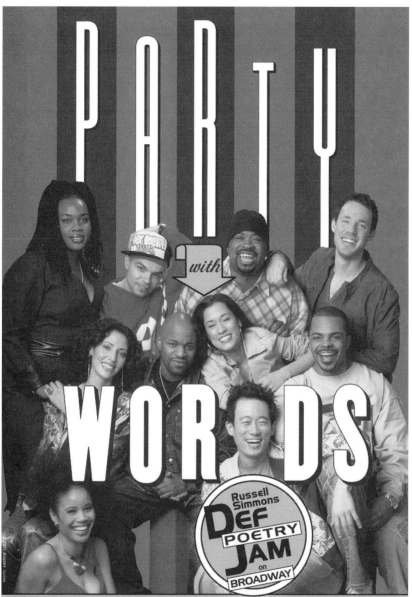

Hip-hop on Broadway: Russell Simmons Def Poetry Jam.

are a testament to culture, having the power to transcend the deepest of conflicts and to elevate thinking and possibilities. The hip-hop industry has sustained its artistry while simultaneously appealing to the commercial capitalist mentality. How can we draw from hip-hop's example?

1. Research/Product

As I stated earlier, it's important when embracing a philosophy of audience development to research not only your *potential* audiences but also your *existing* audiences. What is their relationship to your product, your institution and your mission? Do they feel a sense of ownership in the work? When you put together a campaign for a specific audience, you have to evaluate their lifestyles, how and where they live, their likes and dislikes and their spending power.

Let's take a look at urban market research. In one example, two enterprising young men introducing a new beer hosted more than 100 promotional events in clubs and bars to boost product awareness. On-site promotions educate, create awareness and allow consumers to sample the product. Many advertising and marketing mavens rely on focus groups and surveys for most of their market research. This can be expensive. A grassroots approach is less expensive and can be equally effective.

Urban youth are savvy consumers and can tell if the product is fake or doesn't fit their needs. They long for a sense of belonging, so your message should make them feel that by purchasing your product or service they are included. You have to welcome them into the store and make them know that you want to do business with them. You must align yourself with the ways they identify themselves. In *Black Enterprise* (December 1999), Raymond O'Neal, Jr., former Executive Vice President of Vibe/SPIN Ventures, says, "Urban youth consumers don't respond to messages that are heavy-handed or condescending." Merely seeing Tiger Woods on the golf course or the Williams sisters on the tennis court sends the message to young black people that they are welcome.

2. The Business of Art

Many small arts organizations say they don't have the resources to build audiences. I believe they can't afford *not* to. Arts organizations should consider creating entrepreneurial programs that will generate streams of income, such as merchandising and sponsorships. They should hire development consultants when necessary to research and prepare proposals that are competitive and reflect the artistic brilliance demonstrated onstage or on the walls of their galleries. They should develop sustainable programs, activities that extend beyond the immediate and that have the potential for solid growth.

When I was still at DTH, we were contacted by Bloomingdale's—they wanted to feature the company's ballerinas in advertisements for a new line of cocktail dresses. We negotiated a fee of $500 per dancer—nothing to laugh at for a one-day shoot in 1988—and DTH benefited from a full-page ad in the *New York Times* featuring the dancers. Fortuitously, it was around the time of our New York performance season, so we were able to promote our shows as well.

The Broadway cast of *Noise/Funk* was often called upon to do fashion shows during Fashion Week in New York; they also introduced a new watch at the Tourneau store on Fifth Avenue. Surveys found that the show's audiences had strong European and Asian constituencies, many of whom spoke little English and didn't understand most of the cultural references in the show—but they had a point of identification. Did Japanese youth, with their lack of ghettos, culture wars and racial disharmony, perceive hip-hop as the soundtrack to international fashion? Blackness, embodied in Africa medallions, baggy jeans and even $500 dreadlock treatments and skin darkeners, are commodities on the streets of Tokyo. My former hairdresser would regale me with stories of her salon in Tokyo, with high-paying customers patiently waiting for lock extensions. Is this what the Japanese audience saw in *Noise/Funk*?

3. Diversify Staff

Diversify your staff and board. Hire people who mirror the communities you are committed to developing into audience members. Audience development is a long-term commitment that requires a champion. Build an audience development department, or have at least one full-time staff person devoted to it—it is not a part-time job. The effort should parallel all your institution's sales efforts, including marketing, press and box office. Create a holistic way of approaching and nurturing your new constituents. If you are unwilling or unable to hire the recommended personnel, then consider the following steps: Learn more about other cultures by reading about, spending time in, and observing them without judgment; initiate dialogue about the differences you observe; and conduct culture-specific focus groups to get more information.

4. Diversify Staff—Exactly What Does It Mean?

The lack of diversity in marketing continues to be a problem. Beyond the arts, the overall statistics measuring diversity in the corporate marketing industry are dismal. Heide Gardner, Vice President of Diversity and Strategic Programs for the New York–based American Advertising Federation, notes, "The most recent study, done by the Boston Ad Club in 1997, showed that only 4% of employees and less than 1% of managers in the U.S. ad industry were ethnic minorities."

There has been a lot of buzz about recognizing cultural nuances in marketing and honoring these traditions. This does not deal, however, with developing these customers on a long-term basis, nor does it incorporate the ongoing needs of that particular group. An article by Lisa Bertagnoli in *Marketing News* (January 2001), notes the following: "Many marketers point out that not being of a particular race or ethnicity doesn't necessarily translate into a lack of cultural understanding. Similarly, hailing from a certain ethnic group doesn't guarantee effective marketing campaigns targeted at those consumers. Just because you're of the culture, it doesn't make you an expert . . . Companies often make the mistake of hiring a person of color out of college and thinking they have their bases covered."

This brings to mind an experience I had on tour with *Noise/Funk*. In one of our tour cities, the presenters engaged an African American staff member, thinking he would be a perfect liaison with the local community. After a brief conversation, I realized he had an elitist and condescending attitude toward people who lived in the nearby projects and felt reaching out to them would not be worth the effort. He thought the focus should be on professionals and leaders of the community. My dilemma was whether to inform the presenter about the nuances of selecting appropriate staff and risk cutting off their efforts, or find a limited way to work with this person and identify another community liaison. I did the latter.

In such cases, I often caution my students and clients to select a voice from the community, a person who walks among the people with fluidity, whether they are lower-, middle- or upper-class. These subtleties may seem tiring, but it is just this sense of detail that will ensure a change in someone's perception and his or her experience of the arts and culture.

So is it a question of ethnicity or skill? Julia Huang, Chief Executive Officer of InterTrend Communications, Inc., notes, "It doesn't matter who I'm working with, as long as that marketer is interested in succeeding in reading the Asian market." Tony Ruiz, a partner at Vidal Partnership, a Hispanic communications agency in New York, agrees: "The person who has experience is the better ambassador."

I disagree with both. All my experiences have told me that people who feel excluded need to see a mirror of themselves extending the invitation. I think we should be cautious not to ghettoize within organizations, so that audience development professionals are perceived able to only market effectively within target communities. The point is to diversify the experience, not just the audience. This was my task at The Public: to institutionalize the experience of diversity by claiming it within every department of the organization.

5. Increase Audience Development Staff

There is a great new legion of audience development specialists working in arts organizations of all kinds.

City Theatre of Pittsburgh, a company that is dedicated to "contemporary plays of substance and ideas that engage and challenge diverse audiences," hired its first Community Relations Director, Jeannine Foster-McKelvia, in February 2001. The Managing Director, David Jobin, noted, "The new position was created to help fulfill the theatre's mission to 'engage and challenge diverse audiences.'"

As discussed in the last chapter, for the past five years, the Metropolitan Museum of Art has had an Audience Development Specialist, Donna Sutton, whose strategy has been to target national multicultural organizations, encouraging them to bring their membership to the museum to enjoy its vast and varied collections and to become members. She produces a quarterly newsletter and hosts special events encouraging museum membership. As Community Liaison at Pittsburgh's Carnegie Museum of Art, Deborah Starling Sims's primary objective is to generate more cultural and economic diversity for the museum as a whole. Toward that end, she has created a program called "Stepping Stones," designed to reach a broader audience, including lower-income families. It encourages children to make quarterly visits to CMA and participate in existing Saturday programming. While there, they can take self-guided tours of the permanent or temporary collection currently on view.

This is just a sampling of the increasing number of cultural institutions that recognize the value of investing in staff to cultivate new audiences.

6. Programming

Create programming that reflects the interests and culture of your target audiences. Allow it to be a collaborative process. Nurture and cultivate your new relationships carefully and lovingly. Follow up every step of the way; continue cultivation until new audiences are bringing other constituents to your events.

The 1990s marked a huge jump in culture consumption. In a *Wall Street Journal* article ("From Small Towns to Big Cities, America Is Becoming Cultured," September 21, 1998), Douglas A. Blackmon notes that historic levels of wealth, educational attainment and cultural exposure have converged over the past decade in such a way that the lowest common denominator of American culture is rising rapidly. "Hardly any place is as remote as it once was. Contrary to the wails of many cultural critics, middle-class, mainstream Americans have become, simply put, sophisticated." He quotes interesting statistics: "Nearly 27 million people attended theatrical stage shows during the 1997–98 season—almost 60% of them outside New York . . . according to The League of American Theatres & Producers . . . More than 110 American symphonies . . . have been founded since 1980, according to the American Symphony Orchestra League. Opera attendance, spurred by the use of computerized supertitles that translate lyrics, climbed to nearly 7.5 million in the 1996–97 season, up 34% from 1980 . . . Book sales are at unprecedented levels, with about 430 million more purchased in 1995 than in 1982." Blackmon goes on: "There is also little evidence that the wealth-driven trends marking the shift in cultural tastes have touched the enormous minority of the population who haven't shared significantly in the U.S. economic boom . . . Fundamental economic shifts are indeed fueling the cultural transformation . . . Wealth has grown significantly in the last two decades and permeated more deeply into the middle- and blue-collar classes." Ethnic shifts, though still small in most places, are subtly but broadly altering American perspectives. Blackmon also credits airline deregulation, expanding international flight schedules, cable television and the internet with bringing about an explosion of cultural influences.

Then came September 11, 2001. Everything changed. The arts and culture industry has yet to fully recover. There have been significant declines in attendance and funding. Many small arts organizations have ceased to exist. Museums, theatre and opera memberships have declined across the board. People are hesitant about making long-term commitments, and those that are financially capable of memberships are holding on to their resources. The result is smaller-scale productions, reduced staffs and hours of operation, and a more creative approach to programming. For example, The Public produced only one Shakespeare in the Park summer production (as opposed to the two or three of previous years) until 2005, and the Brooklyn Museum is closed two weeks in the summer.

7. Broad Definitions

Defining audience development requires a broad-minded perspective that takes into account the specific needs of particular communities. It is therefore not limited to ethnicity, but in fact may include age, geography, class and financial status. Enabling the physically challenged (in New York State alone there are 2 million people in this category) to attend arts and cultural events is of increasing importance. They need to be invited and engaged, and facilities have to adapt their lobbies to accommodate wheelchairs, make sure their infrared listening devices are working, and prepare large-print programs, at the very least. Set goals so that you can measure your effectiveness. Understand that it may take time before you see results. Allow 6–12 months for planting seeds. This way, when the time comes to promote your show, local businesses and organizations will be glad to support you because you have been supporting them.

8. Building Communities

Talk to your communities. Be as creative as you can in enhancing and expanding the ways you communicate. If you are expecting them to participate, what are you giving back? Be active in your neighborhood: sit on local boards or neighborhood associations. If there are block associations, contests or festivals, place yourself in the arena so that you'll gain knowledge and support and have visibility.

Look for neglected or often overlooked groups. Offer discount packages or flexible hours. I know of one theatre in New York, the Jean Cocteau Repertory, that offered matinee performances for employees of neighboring hospitals. A great idea.

Julie Franz Peeler, National Director of Chicago's pioneering Arts Marketing Center, has continuously presented opportunities for not-for-profit arts organizations to explore ways of diversifying Chicago's audiences for arts and culture. Her organization, which was founded in 1996 through a collaborative effort by the Arts & Business Council of Chicago, the John D. and Catherine T. McArthur Foundation and the Sara Lee Foundation, is committed to audience development and has published several studies and reports documenting lessons learned from Chicago's cultural community. Joan Gunzberg, Executive Director of Arts & Business Council of Chicago, notes in "Diversifying Chicago's Arts Audiences": "The growing shift toward non-Caucasian populations becoming a majority in Chicago, and in most cities throughout the country, is a trend that will continue to grow at an even more dramatic rate in the new millennium . . . It is essential for organizations of the future to appreciate how this sociological phenomenon enriches and impacts the arts and cultural sector of our society. For the theatre, dance, music or museum patron who looks around at the audience, more likely than not s/he notices a consistency in the group, be it by age or race or ethnicity . . . For future-oriented organizations, the diversification of their audiences is essential to their long-term survival."

Developed from the model established by the Arts Marketing Center, the National Arts Marketing Project is part of a partnership between the New York–based Arts & Business Council and Chicago's Arts & Business Council. Funded by American Express, it provides $25,000 grants to cultural organizations that demonstrate the ability to craft and implement an effective audience development plan over a three-year period. This project provides eight days of mandatory training for executive directors and marketing directors from thirty-two select organizations from around the country. This mix of performing and visual arts organization directors participates in a crash M.B.A. course in arts marketing. As one of the lecturers since the project's inception, I have been able to observe firsthand the value of this program in polishing marketing and audience development skills for executive directors and marketing directors across the country.

9. Educate Marketers

If the classes aren't being taught, if the skills don't exist—teach them yourself! I recognized years ago the lack of people of color in executive- and senior-level arts administration positions. I submitted a proposal to Fordham University, where I served as an adjunct professor until 2001, asking them to support a certificate program that provides executive-level training for a select group of arts administrators of color in New York. The program has been in operation for three semesters to date, with alumni from major cultural organizations as well as small companies. The curriculum consists of a four-week intensive seminar on marketing, fund-raising, legal strategy, strategic planning and management. At the end of the session, the participants receive a certificate and return to their organizations with a stronger set of skills, which should enhance their market value and skill base.

Since 1993 I have been teaching at many colleges, including Fordham, New York University, Brooklyn College and, more recently, at Columbia University as an adjunct professor, because I feel there is a lack of humanism and connection to diverse audiences in the marketing of art and culture.

One way of promoting education is to create your own professional organization. "Sapphire" is an informal support group of expert marketers and corporate executives that arose out of a need to provide marketing support for an emerging spoken-word performer, Sarah Jones. Ms. Jones had worked with Isisara Bey at Sony BMG Music, who invited me and our mutual friends, Monique Martin and Tracey Mendelsohn (both of whom are highly experienced marketers and producers in the field of art and culture), to the meeting. We provided Ms. Jones with a marketing plan and held continuing consultations over a six-month period to advise her on management and marketing strategies. She is now a formidable talent and presence in the spoken-word and theatre communities, with a one-person show headed for Broadway in fall 2005. After this success, we decided to provide marketing support for ourselves to enhance each of our own career objectives. We met quarterly over a three-year period, advising each other on how to be leaders in our field. Today, all four of us are quite accomplished in our professions: Isisara Bey is Vice President for Corporate Affairs at Sony BMG Music; Monique Martin is the producer of a highly successful series, *Soul Erotica*, onstage and on HBO; and Tracey Mendelsohn is President of QuickSilver Entertainment, with clients in the commercial, sports and film industries. All three women continue to give of their time and resources to support arts and culture in their respective arenas.

10. Cross-Fertilization

What is cross-fertilization? Do we have to do it? What is its value? We may be striving for audiences to naturally and organically (because they trust the product and the process) engage in exploring the stories of people different from themselves as part of their day-to-day sampling of arts and culture, or we may want them to immerse themselves in a particular cultural institution. These moves can't be forced. The first step is to be familiar with your neighborhood. The next is to reach out to diverse groups.

Cynthia Mayeda, Deputy Director for Institutional Advancement for the Brooklyn Museum, stated at a seminar in October 2001 that she was coming to believe that people who came to the museum for its "First Saturdays" series (a free program of art and entertainment) did not necessarily have to become members. If they came for the free music and fun time, that was great—the point was that they came to the museum. When this was accomplished, the goal was fulfilled. This does not preclude museum-goers from furthering their relationship with the museum, but it also does not negate the value of people coming simply to enjoy a "First Saturdays" event.

I am often asked, "Did you experience any crossover with your audiences? Did your target market choose mainstream productions as well as those that reflected their culture?" This question implies that the success of our outreach efforts depends on our audience members' experiencing several different kinds of culture, which I believe is an invalid judgment. Frankly, I have found that the audiences we are trying to reach are not starving culturally; they have made choices about how they want to be entertained and how they want to experience culture. Our job is to provide access to different possibilities, ones that we believe will enhance their cultural understanding. But to believe that a group is deprived because they choose not to experience our more traditional art and cultural offerings goes against the core philosophy of audience development. At The Public we found that the majority of audiences of color would first choose the show that most closely reflected their own culture, and then would usually move on to enjoying Shakespeare, for example. Sometimes they would venture to sample a new playwright, but their strongest impulse was to see stories of themselves.

11. Financial Support

Funders should take note that artists need time to think and develop projects—so, while it's important to be assured that an artist or organization is financially stable and can utilize a gift in an intelligent manner, the financial health of the recipient should not preclude them from receiving a grant if the purpose of the project is clear and creative. Artists need time to research the projects and to document their work. Let's expand the definition of who is worthy of receiving money. Let's formulate think tanks for arts organizations to brainstorm on strategies for economic success.

An interesting issue is raised when we examine urban markets and expectations for funding. While working on *Harlem Song*, the producers were positioned to receive funding from several national corporations. The funders were hesitant to give the money, however, until they felt that the black community, particularly black corporate leadership, was invested in the project. That happened—but only just before the show was scheduled for a premature closing—when investment from a black advertising agency signaled the release of the promised corporate funds, enabling the show to complete its scheduled run. This is an important point: Whose responsibility is it to sustain the growth and development of urban art? How can we create a more solid commitment from ethnic businesses to invest in their own art and cultural organizations?

Woodie King, Jr., Founder and Producing Director of New Federal Theatre, states in *Black Masks* magazine (August 2003) that "black artists have a responsibility to court black businesses," and proposes that if at least ten of the top one hundred black businesses gave $2,500 to twenty black not-for-profit art organizations each year, it would create a funding pool of $250,000. He cites the solid support from the black church community as key to the financial success of Vy Higginsen's *Mama, I Want to Sing*, which grossed $8.3 million in 1998.

12. Black Talk Radio

James Mtume, a member of KISS-FM's talk team and a Grammy Award–winning composer, said in a *New York Times* article ("Talking Back on Black Talk Radio . . ." January 21, 2000) that there is tremendous growth potential in black talk radio: "I think black talk radio is a sleeping giant ready to blow up." A former host at WLIB, Imhotep Gary Byrd, added: "Black talk radio is the drum of the community," discussing fundamental issues about race. Why can't this become a venue to discuss arts and culture? Let's take it to another level.

13. 21st Century Audience Development

Developing audiences for the arts is not a new concept, but the arts and culture of our society are just waking up to this. New managers are now paying attention to the dynamics of community. Whether you are a small, ethnic-based organization or a Broadway producer, the issue is identical: Tapping into an unrealized market that can increase your profit margin and everyone's cultural awareness.

14. Independent Films

In March 2001, film director Jim McKay approached me to build an audience development effort for the release of his film, *Our Song*. It tells the story of three multicultural teenage girls coming of age in Brooklyn. Set against the backdrop of the Jackie Robinson Steppers Marching Band, the film follows these girls as they face the challenges of growing up in a world filled with uncertainty, risk and, ultimately, hope.

Under the auspices of my consulting company, we applied (and expanded on) many of the strategies used in our theatre experience, targeting audiences in Brooklyn, Harlem, Queens and the Bronx. The launch event for the film was an outdoor barbecue, attended by more than 1,500 people, at the school where the film was shot in Brooklyn. We distributed *Our Song* bookmarks throughout the public library system and in Barnes & Noble bookstores. We arranged for free community screenings at the Harlem Police Athletic League community center; Planned Parenthood; The Door, a counseling crisis intervention center; and The Point, a multicultural center in the Bronx. We hired a street flyer distribution team that covered many of the summer cultural events and targeted neighborhood businesses.

A booth at the Black Expo in June allowed us to collect more than 5,000 names and email addresses, and to distribute CDs, bookmarks and flyers. A number of people had already seen the film and came over to share their comments with us. It was amazing. The next day, we sent an email out to everyone thanking them for stopping by the booth and reminding them to see the film (if they hadn't) and to tell their friends about it.

We presented a list of local African American and Latino media outlets for ad buys, and the producers coordinated their work with our promotional efforts. Because many of the smaller media sources were rarely approached with cash for an ad buy, they were all the more interested in covering the film. The fact that its cast was multicultural helped bring us significant coverage in these papers, which then supported our audience development efforts. There was synchronicity here.

Partly as a result of these grassroots, coordinated efforts, the film grossed more than $200,000 during the first two months of its New York run, which was outstanding for this intimate type of movie. There was an awareness and openness by Jim McKay to find a new way of reaching a targeted multicultural group of teens and young adults. There was also investment and commitment from the producers to implement our recommendations. Together, we turned this small film event into a major success story for the filmmakers and community.

15. On Broadway

Since working on Anna Deavere Smith's 1994 Broadway production of *Twilight: Los Angeles, 1992*, I have been involved in developing audiences of color for Broadway. After the financial success of *Noise/Funk*, producers became even more aware of the value of courting these communities. I have recently been responsible for audience development for *Russell Simmons Def Poetry Jam*; August Wilson's *Gem of the Ocean* and *Ma Rainey's Black Bottom* with Whoopi Goldberg; Tony Kushner and Jeanine Tesori's *Caroline, or Change*; the Apollo's *Jackie Wilson Story* and *Hairspray*. In each case, the mandate was to identify, engage and promote tickets to the African American community. We utilized many of the ideas described in this book. Our greatest success—always—was when working in partnership with community organizations.

Hairspray is an interesting example, because it is a production in which the involvement of African Americans is not so obvious. But, we set up a three-year plan to engage these audience members. We began by building a presence within the community, appearing at numerous street fairs, outdoor festivals and events that reached our target market. We continued to build on our efforts.

There are other urban marketing companies being utilized for target audiences on Broadway. *Flower Drum Song* retained an Asian American marketing company, Factor, Inc., to target that demographic. Factor, Inc. was successful in generating more than $500,000 in ticket sales and through special events tied to the community.

16. National Awareness

Since 1993, I have regularly lectured and provided workshops to a multitude of arts service, education, performing and visual arts institutions across the nation. Collectively, senior staff, board members and marketing and education directors share one objective: Diversify their audiences. I am deeply encouraged by this awareness. Nationally, this work is still in its pioneer stages, but I am quite confident that as we increase staffing and programming, the efforts will increase and reach the deepest pockets of our country. With the rapidly changing demographics in the U.S., we have no choice but to design strategies and build partnerships that welcome diverse audiences.

Conclusion

"Come to the edge," he said. They said, "We
are afraid." "Come to the edge," he said. They
came. He pushed them . . . and they flew.

—Guillaume Apollinaire

Dance, theatre and music have changed my life. As a former dancer
I understand the passion, the need, the hunger and the drive of the
artist. Seeing my first ballet at the age of five; becoming a professional
dancer, teacher, and then practicing attorney; serving as arts administrator, college professor, lecturer and writer—at the center of all these
careers has been my love, my passion, for the arts. I have transferred
that love and experience to building audiences for other artists.

I want every person to be given an opportunity to experience
and develop a love for the arts. To do that, we need to create access for
diverse audiences, breaking down those barriers that keep people outside. I believe that when cultural institutions actively engage in developing audiences, the collective effort positively impacts each one of
us—a wave takes form, and entire communities become empowered.
The arts are essential, and since 9/11 they have become even more
necessary, as has the critical importance of community and the need to

respect each other's differences. The arts are the best tool we have for social change. When we experience great works of art—in that moment—we transcend our differences and feel a common humanity. The arts cultivate nonviolence, trust, solidarity, community and breadth of mind. As Daisaku Ikeda, President of Soka Gakkai International (a lay organization promoting peace, culture and education based on the teachings of Nichiren Buddhism), has stated: "Cultured people value peace and lead others to a world of beauty, hope and bright tomorrows."

The first event for The Public's 2001–2002 season was scheduled for October 7, 2001. It was to be a reading with novelist/social critic John Edgar Wideman and poet Rita Dove, celebrating *Callaloo's* (an African American literary journal edited by Charles Rowell) twenty-fifth anniversary. Because of the timing, George C. Wolfe, Charles and I wondered if we should hold the event at all; the city was still in shock. After much thought and discussion, we decided to go forward. We believed so strongly in the healing power of the arts that we knew those who chose to come would greatly benefit from joining together that day. Slowly the reservations trickled in, and on that Sunday 250 people came. They were relieved to have somewhere to go during that tough time—a home where art could transcend their lives.

Charles opened up the program with a statement reflecting the need for peace. Then Rita read some of her extraordinary poems. Her words served as a balm for the deep pain we all shared. John Edgar shared witty passages from his latest novel. The humor was very refreshing. I have never seen the healing power of the arts effect people so directly as I did on that day. Afterward people laughed and cried and talked and talked and talked. It was an incredible day—it was about our audience, about giving them what they needed.

Strangely enough, since 9/11, my business has increased. Arts and cultural organizations want to know: "How do we engage a diverse community?" Throughout my twenty-five-year career in audience development, I have never experienced such a fervent effort to work with this issue. This is promising. Yet at the time when the need for cultural outreach is greatest, we are experiencing severe budget cuts through-

Alvin Ailey American Dance Theater's Clifton Brown.

out the country. This makes our job very difficult, and we must work more creatively than ever to meet our goals, engaging presenters, producers, the community and the artists—everybody—in our quest.

Understanding and then removing the barriers that prevent your target market from being engaged are of primary importance. Building audiences is not an easy task, yet our world today demands that we make the effort. Once you implement the Ten Tools of Audience Development you can effectively *sustain* relationships that will continually support the growth of arts and culture in your community. Forming a community of audience development specialists can only enrich the field and the product. An infiltration of these experts would surely encourage more cross-cultural collaborations and create new forms of access to the performing arts. Meeting, crafting projects, forming partnerships are essential elements of this work. By listening carefully and setting aside our preconceived ideas, we can discover new ways to engage our communities.

Artists and audiences must share their vision with each other. The arts and the audience should mirror each other. With my students across the country, I have shared my experiences and strategies, leading them to discover their own creative approaches to diversifying and expanding audiences. Fortunately, many of them are now working in arts organizations and are applying what they have learned. The conversation with all of them continues to be proactive. Their commitment encourages me to continually find new ways to extend the invitation.

Acknowledged as the nation's foremost expert in audience diversification by the Arts & Business Council, DONNA WALKER-KUHNE, an accomplished arts administrator and educator, has devoted her professional career to increasing the accessibility and connection to the arts for our nation's rapidly growing multicultural population.

Since 1984, Ms. Walker-Kuhne has been President of Walker International Communications Group. She conducts seminars and workshops, and provides marketing consultation services to arts organizations, performing and visual artists, dance companies, Broadway and Off-Broadway productions, and other not-for-profit organizations. Her clients include the Romare Bearden Foundation; Alvin Ailey American Dance Theater; the Bill T. Jones/Arnie Zane Dance Company; the Broadway hit: *Hairspray*; *Three Mo' Tenors*; the Columbia University Arts Initiative; the Apollo Theater; Sony Music; WNYC Radio; the Arts & Business Council and Dance/USA. She was recently an Associate Producer for the critically acclaimed production of George C. Wolfe's *Harlem Song* at the world-famous Apollo Theater.

From 1993 through 2002, Ms. Walker-Kuhne served as the Director of Marketing and Audience Development for The Public Theater in New York City. While there, she originated a range of audience development activities that reached thousands of children, students and adults in multicultural communities throughout the city's five boroughs. Her work to reach New York City public school students included a successful group ticket sales initiative, which enabled more than 8,000 students to attend performances at The Public Theater.

As The Public Theater's National Coordinator for Community Outreach, Ms. Walker-Kuhne completed a national 32-city tour of *Bring in 'Da Noise, Bring in 'Da Funk*. For the tour, she effectively increased audiences across the country by more than 20% through community-based marketing campaigns in more than 25 urban markets. She also developed "Bring in 'Da Kids," an innovative outreach and educational program that brought 20,000 children to the show, and involved more than 33,000 students in a variety of related programs.

Prior to her work at The Public Theater, Ms. Walker-Kuhne was the Director of Marketing for Dance Theatre of Harlem (1984–93), where she created and implemented the highly successful public relations and marketing campaign for their unprecedented tour of Johannesburg, South Africa (1992), and all marketing and audience development for the company's tour in Cairo. While at DTH, she increased box office sales by 45%. To aid in this endeavor, she originated and guided DTH's "National Audience Development Task Force." In 1992, her work significantly contributed to DTH's successful New York season at Lincoln Center and the Brooklyn Academy of Music.

Before working for DTH, Ms. Walker-Kuhne began her career in arts administration as Managing Director for the Thelma Hill Performing Arts Center in Brooklyn.

In 1998, she became the first American invited by the National Arts Council of Singapore to teach an extensive marketing workshop. She was selected by *Theater* magazine as one of the top fifty people to be a force in theatre's future. She was also presented with the "keys" to the City of Miami, and was awarded a 2002 Dynamic Women Award by Councilman Nick Perry of Brooklyn. In 2003, she became the first American asked by the Australian Council on the Arts to do a lecturing tour on "Ethnic Diversity for Arts Organizations." In 2004, she was honored with the Pioneering Women in Theater Award by the Black Public Relations Society of Greater New York, where she received citations from Manhattan Borough President, C. Virginia Fields; Brooklyn City Councilmember, Yvette Clarke; and U.S. Congressman, Major R. Owens.

Ms. Walker-Kuhne is an Adjunct Professor instructing in Marketing the Arts at Brooklyn College, Columbia University and New York University. She was nominated for the Ford Foundation's "2001 Leadership for a Changing World Fellowship," for an intensive certificate program she developed and offered at Fordham University entitled, "Arts Marketing and Program Development for Multicultural Arts Administrators."

She is a keynote speaker for numerous national organizations including Dance/USA, Theatre Communications Group, the Coming Up Taller Leadership Conference and the Arts & Business Council.

Ms. Walker-Kuhne's career began as Assistant Corporation Council for the State of New York, while she danced professionally on a part-time basis with the Najwa Dance Corps. She received her Juris Doctor from Howard University School of Law in Washington, D.C., and her B.A from Loyola University in Chicago.